# GUIDE TO
# SURVIVING LIFE

## by

## Myron J. Kukla

Library of Congress Cataloging-in Publication Data
Kukla, Myron J.
ISBN  0-0665606-1-2

All of the articles that appear in this book were originally published in
*The Lakeshore/Grand Rapids Press*.

Published in the United States by
Lockport Books
Old Orchard Place
273 Lakeshore Dr.
Holland, MI  49424

Printed in the United States of America on acid-free paper.

Cover design by Alan Shepard.

**DEDICATION**
*For my family and friends.*

Inspirational Quote:

"It's a bit embarrassing to have been concerned
with the human problem all one's life and find out
at the end that one has no more to offer by way
of advice than 'Try to be a little kinder.' "

ALDOUS HUXLEY

Also by Myron J. Kukla

*Confessions of a Baby Boomer: Memories of things I haven't forgotten yet*

*Something in the Blood*

# CONTENTS

# INTRODUCTION

I have a confession to make. This book isn't really a guide to surviving life. If life were so simple that you could just write down a few rules and clever sayings which any dummy could follow to be happy, your HMO would just hand you a one-page Xerox set of directions on "how to live" at birth and then send you annual updates on the Internet.

Actually, surviving life in all its weird and delightful forms is too complex to summarize in a book -- any book -- whether it's "Ten Steps to Instant Sanity," "The Golden Rules for Financial Independence," or a 12-point guide on "How to do the Polka." I know because I've read them all and I'm still crazy, broke and can't do the Polka.

It's no wonder we tend to look to books and guides and gurus to tell us what to do. Today, we have to deal with things our parents never prepared us for like fitness centers and 'hip hop' music. We have to look good forever, be a tireless worker bee on the job, a creative lover in bed, a sensitive partner in relation-ships, and a master of complex electronic gadgets that change every other week. Plus, we need to be caring and devoted parents prepared to raise intelligent children who will go off to college and make us proud, and then, just when they become interesting, they go and start their own lives.

Today it doesn't matter whether you are a male or female, from Venus, Mars or Climax, Michigan. Life is hard for every-one. We have to deal every day with our messed up childhoods where we had to learn to read using Phonics, survive book bag envy in grade school, and lousy family vacations at a time when our only childhood role models where Hugh Hefner and the Three Stooges. And our moms, God bless them, cured our ills with their home remedies and instilled in us the need to eat our vegetables, not run with scissors and wear clean underwear for accidents.

And, even though we're grown now, working through our fears of personal inadequacy and dependence on prescription drugs that make you feel better but could also turn you into a frog under certain conditions, we have to appear normal and confident while worrying about killer bees, how we will look at our class reunion, and why our glasses and car keys don't stay where we put them any more.

This is not a book to help you with your problems. It is a guide to show you how to laugh at life and the things in life that make it so stressful. It is a guide to help men understand what women want for Valentine's Day and help women understand why guys can't find things at the grocery store. It is a source of enlightenment on why Christmas letters from your friends make you feel you have wasted your life, and how telemarketers can bring a little joy into your world.

So, read, enjoy and learn. For this is your guide to surviving life, my way.

Myron J. Kukla

# Chapter I
# SURVIVING GOOD HEALTH

*Trying to stay healthy has become the number one priority for people in mid-life. You will find in this chapter realistic tips on surviving miracle diets, wonder drugs, and outdoor sports — all of which can kill you. I also deal with the issue of how much exercise do you really need to stay alive?*

*There seems to be some rule in medicine these days that drug names have to start with either an A, V, X or Z. Seriously, when was the last time you heard a doctor prescribe "cough syrup?"*

# SURVIVING MIRACLE DRUGS

The people who keep track of statistics, say that every seven seconds a baby boomer is turning "50" these days. All I can say to them is "happy birthday" and welcome to middle age.

Well, it is middle age if you're planning on living to be 100. And chances are you can reach that goal if you look after your health, don't overeat, drink plenty of bottled water and take your drugs every day.

Just like 30 years ago, when most of us baby boomers were in our teens or early 20s, the big topic of discussion these days among us wilting "flower children" is drugs. The only difference between then and now is, today we can talk openly about our drug use and no one is going to arrest us.

The other evening, I was out with a few friends who are at the half-century mark and the conversation turned to the prescription drugs we are taking for what ails us. Within minutes, we sounded like a group of pharmaceutical reps at a sales convention.

"I'm taking about 100 milligrams of Antebellumfacade daily, along with a prescription for Zigotafone, plus a morning dose of Vigeroplantfood and I'm feeling much better."

"Well, my doctor has me on Aerosmithafarb, Xylophonigraph and Zweibachitus for the same problem."

## A TO Z MEDICATION

There seems to be some rule in medicine these days that drug names have to start with either an A, V, X or Z. Seriously, when was the last time you heard a doctor prescribe "cough syrup?" Now it's, "I'm going to have you take some Vermaloxozephercal to cure that cough."

And it's not just the drug names that are confusing. Have you ever read the disclaimers that come along with some of the drugs out today? It's like trying to read a medical journal typeset by munchkins. I swear they put 20 pages of information on a piece of paper the size of a gum wrapper using dust-speck printing that no one who needs to take the drug can possibly read without a magnifying glass.

Actually, after getting out my magnifying glass and reading a number of these disclaimers, I realized that all of the pharmaceutical companies say the same thing in the fine print which is this. "Be forewarned, under certain circumstances, this drug may kill you or possibly turn you into a frog."

## SCARY WARNINGS

I really don't think people should read warnings about the drugs they have to take. The warnings are too scary. For example, I got a new prescription the other day and the following is a short description of the fun things the company knows can actually happen to me on my new medication.

It reads: "There have been reports of serious, sometimes fatal, reactions including hyperthermia, rigidity, myoclonus, autonomic instability with possible rapid fluctuations of vital signs, mental status changes that include extreme agitation progressing to delirium and coma."

Makes me wonder whether controlling that facial twitch I have is really worth delirium, coma and death. Not to mention that I could also wind up turning into a frog.

Another drug I'm taking tells me possible side effects include heart arrhythmia, congestive heart failure, a cerebral embolism or, in extreme cases, I could find myself "standing on a street corner quacking like a duck."

The popular drug Zyban, which helps people quit smoking, advises that in addition to sudden seizures, those taking the drug are also eligible to have "anaphylactoid/anaphylactic reaction characterized by pruritus, urticaria, angioedema and dyspnea," all of which requires "immediate medical treatment."

3

If I knew what those things were and could possibly pronounce them for a physician in an emergency room, it would probably sound like this.  "Dr. I think I'm having an attack of aphids, prurient interests, angiedickensen and dippsydoodle from my medication. Please help me. Quack, quack."

## REAL MEN DON'T READ

Actually, men are pretty safe from having to worry about these problems. If they are like me,  most men don't even read the list of possible side effects that comes with medications. I usually just take a quick look at the label on the pill bottle. It will say "take three times a day with...." That's about as far as I get.

Whether I have to take it with food, water or harsh detergents makes no difference to me.  The reason for this is that at my age, I'm usually adding any new medication to medicines I already take.  If I had to sort them all out and  take one pill with water and one with food and one with marshmallows, I'd never get anything done. So, I usually put them all in my hand in the morning and just gulp them down at once and hope they don't kill me.

Women, though, are different in that regard. They actually read all the information on a drug they are about to take, including the possible side effects.  Then, being forewarned, they don't take the medication.

A typical woman will read a medicine label and go: "Oh, I'm supposed to be taking Xenawarriorprincess three times a day so I won't get confused and crash into buildings with my car anymore.  But I read the possible side effects, and it might cause me to grow hair on my knuckles, so I won't take it."

On the other hand, I've never know a guy to look at the fine print of any medication warning.  Basically, most of us just scan the material to see if there's any skull and cross bones anywhere and if there's not, we go ahead and take our chances.

I have no doubt that a pharmaceutical company could actually list with the side effects on medication for male pattern baldness a warning that advises "While taking this drug, you may experience a swelling, and possible exploding, of your head. Green fungus will sprout on your earlobes and you could develop an irrational urge to shove pencils up your nose. In some severe cases, you may also turn into a frog."

Most guys taking the medication would just put it on their heads and six months later go, "My hair is growing back again since I started using Zoroastrian, but now I've picked up this green earlobe fungus from somewhere and my head feels like it's going to explode. Can I borrow a pencil? Ribbet."

*Since I started dieting, I have lost exactly 4,228 pounds in 40 years — or the equivalent body mass of 26 fully grown men. Obviously, I didn't lose all this weight through willpower alone.*

# SURVIVING FAD DIETS

Well, it's two weeks into the new year, and if you're like me, you've probably just decided that it wasn't a very good idea to have been eating non-stop since Thanksgiving.

Right now, you are likely planning to start on a diet to get back into shape so you can see your toes again.

Before you start on your diet, though, it is a good idea to get some advice from an expert on the subject. But, since that would probably require you to get up from the couch and waddle over to another piece of furniture near a phone book, the next best thing you could do is read this.

You see, I am a bit of an expert on dieting. In fact, I've been on a diet since I was 7 years old when I split the seams on what was termed in those not-so-politically-correct times as "chubby jeans." I began dieting that day.

Since I started dieting, I have lost exactly 4,228 pounds in 40 years — or the equivalent body mass of 26 fully grown men. Obviously, I didn't lose all this weight through willpower alone.

No, my success in dieting has been as a result of following very carefully formulated, scientifically proven fad diets, all based on some simple principle that can be summarized on the dust cover of diet books with titles like "Losing Weight with the Holistic Flesh-Eating Microbe Diet."

What I've found in my search for escape from the perfect pear-shaped body is that there are basically two ways to lose weight. One is to follow a sensible, well-balanced diet program coupled with regular exercise. This is what most respectable health and nutritional experts recommend, but we all know this healthy method takes too long and usually leaves you hungry enough to eat road kill.

The other approach is to lose weight by following miracle diets, which produce remarkable results eating strange food groups like hot dogs, baby seals and bean dip.

To save you the effort of searching out these miracle diets, I've prepared a summary of some of the more intriguing diets I've come across over the years, plus, a few practical dieting tips I've learned from trial and error.

I've indicated how much you can expect to lose on each diet, some of the drawbacks and typical comments from people who have tried these weight-loss programs.

### THE CABBAGE SOUP DIET

You can eat anything you want on this diet as long as it is cabbage. You can eat cooked cabbage, stewed cabbage, boiled cabbage, baked cabbage, raw cabbage, cabbage with salt, cabbage with pepper, cabbage with salt and pepper, etc. You can expect to lose 8 to 10 pounds a week on this diet. Drawback: No one wants to be around you because you smell like cabbage all the time.

### THE "QUIERO TACO BELL?" DIET

With this diet, you can eat any type of food you want as long as it has been licked first by a Chihuahua. Average weight loss is about 10 pounds per Chihuahua. Typical comments from dieters, "I don't care if he licked it. I'm starving and I'm going to eat it."

### THE PRAYER DIET

On this diet, you pray for seven days to lose weight, taking nothing but water and fruit juices while you pray. In just a week, you will miraculously lose 12 to 20 pounds. The most typical comment of those on the prayer diet is, "I just had a celestial vision of prime rib and garlic mashed potatoes."

## THE SCARSDALE DIET 2

Once considered the best of the diet plans, this diet gives a daily menu of exactly what you may eat to lose anywhere from 5 to 10 pounds a week. The great incentive behind this diet is that if you fail to lose weight on it, a former girlfriend of the diet doctor shows up at your house and shoots you. Typically heard about this diet, "Bang. Thud."

## THE CHOCOLATE DIET

One of the more popular fad diets, the Chocolate Diet was invented by research scientists at Hershey Chocolates. The diet is fairly easy. You must eat two pounds or more of chocolate or other confectionery candy every day for six months. Expect to gain about 40 to 60 pounds on this diet. A very common comment by adherents to this diet is, "Could you please move my leg slightly to the right for me? I just can't seem to lift it anymore."

## THE BEER DIET

This is the same as the Chocolate Diet, only substituting beer for sweets. You simply drink two cases of beer a day and abstain from food. A typical comment from those rigorously following this diet is, "Who am I?"

## THE HERB DIET

This is not really a diet. It's actually a guy named "Herb" who follows you around eating food off your plate. A major drawback to this diet is Herb, who has disgusting table manners.

## TOP 10 DIET TIPS

If you are going to go on one of these diets or other calorie-counting program of your own, here are a few simple dieting rules to help you stay on track:

1. Never start your diet at Pizza Hut.

2. Do not pull a kitchen chair up to the refrigerator to sit on while enjoying a "light snack."

3. Never eat anything larger then your head, at least not in one sitting.

4. Remember, it is counterproductive to your diet to buy foods labeled "low fat" and then put butter on them.

5. Eating a Whopper and fries and then washing it down with Slim Fast makes no sense at all.

6. Do not carry around gravy in a thermos for a quick "pick-me-up."

7. Avoid using whipped cream and sugar sprinkles on granola to make it more appetizing.

8. Celery and carrots are good diet snacks, but not when battered and deep-fried.

9. Foods that are low in calories usually taste like cardboard or celery, unless they are battered and deep-fried

10. The best way to lose weight is to "think thin" and have your mouth wired shut for six months.

*My biceps called me up the other day and said, "You do one more full arm curl extension and we'll fix you so you'll be drinking your coffee through a straw."*

# SURVIVING THE FITNESS CENTER

After you reach 40, you start to ask yourself certain health questions. Things like, "Why is my body making those strange noises?" "What do my feet look like when I'm standing?" and of course the most basic question, "What minimum exercise do I need to do to stay alive?"

After spending the past 30 years believing just doing push-ups from the dinner table would be enough to keep me in shape, I decided to join a physical fitness center. The club I joined is called "Workout Till You Drop." I've been going there for about two months and, I have to say, I feel incredibly exhausted.

This club has a different exercise machine for every muscle in your body. These machines are so specialized, one does nothing but build up my triceps. Triceps, if you aren't aware, are those muscles on the back of your upper arm that you never use except when you want to make holes for ice fishing.

At the fitness center, I am under the guidance of "Rolfe," my personal trainer, who is working on developing my triceps, biceps, deltoids, brachialis and triceratops. Not only am I getting buff, I'm also learning a new language.

After working on these muscles for several weeks under his guidance, I now know exactly where every one of these muscles is located. I know where they're at because they all hurt and they are getting nasty about making them work after a pro-longed period of neglect.

As an example, my biceps called me up the other day and said, "You do one more full arm curl extension and we'll fix you so you'll be drinking your coffee through a straw."

# DESSERT TABLE LA

In the past, I've tried to set my own
walked, usually every day from the house to th
course, back again. I also did cycling. I used to c)
week a whole quarter-mile to the ice cream shop o
And, I've even been known to do laps around the ʋ        .ɔle
before making a selection.

But then I got serious about exercise. I took up jogging
for a while on an indoor track, but I have to admit I found it
pointless. No matter how long I ran, I never seemed to get anywhere.

I tried a spinning class once. Someone told me it was a
great exercise where you work out with a bunch of overweight
people riding stationary bikes. My friend must have been thinking about some other kind of spinning because all my class ever
did was spin sheep's wool into yarn. I didn't build up any muscles
doing this, but I did get a great sweater out of it.

The worst thing I ever tried on my own was the home
aerobics stuff.

I heard about a music exercise tape by some workout guru
named Simmons and bought it. I tried to follow that program,
but I couldn't take all those funny costumes and prancing around
he did.  It was only after I quit that I discovered the exercise tape
I really wanted was done by prancing shiny guy Richard Simmons.
I had bought a Gene Simmons "Kiss" concert tape by mistake.

Because of this mistake I didn't improve myself at all
physically, but I got pretty good at sticking my tongue out and
licking the tip of my nose.

## GETTING BUFFED AND POLISHED

So, now I'm a fully registered member of a health club
where the motto of the place is "No brain, no pain."

All of the staff in this place look like they could bench
press a living room couch.  The rest of us exercise neophytes
look like we could sit on a living room couch. Before he started

Before Rolfe would let me work out on any of the low-impact weight training machines, he showed me some warm-up stretching exercises I had to do at the start of each session. I asked him why they are important, and he explained, "They help you limber up so that if you hurt yourself during exercising, you won't know about it until you go home."

Another exercise tip Rolfe gave me was to always try to work my muscles to the "burn." The burn is the point where you've exercised your muscles until they are crying out in pain, and then you push them even further until your arms fall off.

Although I complain now and then, I'm very pleased with my progress at the fitness center. For one thing, I no longer have to wrap duct tape around my arms to simulate muscles. My deltoids have never looked better. And I've got my abdominal muscles strengthened to the point where I can actually feel I have abdominal muscles.

Working out at a fitness center has changed the way I look at my life and many of my bad habits. Before I started working out there, my usual morning breakfast was three eggs, hash browns, toast and coffee. Today, I start my day with nothing more than two Ibuprofen, an ice pack, Ben Gay and coffee.

*Mowing the grass, clipping hedges, spading the garden,*
*weeding and even digging fence holes are evidently*
*just the ticket to build strong bones*
*as women get older.*

## SURVIVING HEALTH NEWS

I have some wonderful medical news for women who are worried about the bone loss disease osteoporosis, which tends to affect women as they mature. This is also very important news for men who love their spouses and want to see them stay strong and healthy.

Researchers at the University of Arkansas have discovered that doing strenuous yard work is one of the best exercises women can do to build and maintain healthy bones.

The study, which was done by lady researchers I might add, found that women who did yard work and tended gardens had healthier bones than women who did almost any other type of exercise.

This, of course, is wonderful news for women and also great news for their husbands who right now are cheering loudly and giving each other high fives.

I mentioned this discovery to my wife, Madeline, the other day as I danced around the kitchen waving the article around like it was a freshly minted pardon from the governor.

"Let me see that," she said, grabbing the pardon, I mean the article, from my hands.

"This is just the icing on the cake," she said after reading it. "Not only do we women have to bear the children, do the majority of the house work, hold full-time jobs, but now yard work is healthy for us."

"I thought you'd be pleased," I said innocently.

"How come they never do studies that find doing house work is beneficial to men?"

# BUILDS STRONG BONES

The University of Arkansas study found that women who did "heavy and arduous work" in the garden achieved greater bone density than through any other activity. Mowing the grass, clipping hedges, spading the garden, weeding and even digging fence holes are evidently just the ticket to build strong bones as women get older.

In fact, yard work as an exercise ranked higher than dancing, aerobics, swimming or bungie jumping. It's right up there with weight lifting for building strong bones and doesn't produce those unsightly muscle bulges on women.

"Hon, just think about how blessed you are to be living in Michigan, where you can not only do all the gardening and lawn care in summer, but also rake up all the leaves in the fall, clean the gutters, trim tree branches, chop firewood and shovel the snow off the roof this winter," I offered. " You'll be healthy as a horse this year."

"Wait a minute," she objected. "It doesn't say anything about all that other stuff. You're making that up."

"Well, I'm just offering some healthy suggestions to keep your bones strong and firm all year round," I said. "I'm even thinking that cleaning the garage and painting large portions of the house might also fall under beneficial yard work.

"In fact, after reading the article, I decided this would be a good time for you to go out and build that multitiered flower garden you've been wanting for the past five years," I said, offering to go out immediately and order the two tons of decorative bricks and the truckload of topsoil it would require.

She eyed me suspiciously.

"Why the sudden urge to do a project you said was going to be a lot of backbreaking work that would take forever to do?" she asked.

"That's just the point. It's hard and arduous work. And now you can do it because it's scientifically beneficial for you to do hard and arduous work," I said.

# WOMEN GET THE BOOT

"What color wheel barrel and shovel should I get you?" I asked. "How about work boots? Do you want steel toe or the open-front design?"

To be fair, my wife already does the bulk of gardening around our house, putting in and tending a wide array of plants and bushes that every rabbit in the neighborhood likes to come and feast on.

If it were left to me, our yard would be one big square of grass that could be cut in six passes on a riding lawn mower. And our trees would all be evergreens that don't make leaves,

I would also have a snow melt system in the driveway and windows on the house with little wiper blades on them so the windows never needed washing.

It's not that I dislike strenuous yard work. It's just that my bones are plenty strong already and I would just like to share the benefit of this activity by extending a rake to the women of the world.

"Actually, I've been wanting to do the garden wall for a long time" said Madeline. "But healthful as this is going to be for me, I don't think I can do it all myself."

"Don't worry dear, I've got that figured out," I said. "We'll invite over some of our friends and the wives can all pitch in and help you while they build up their bones, too."

"And while we're building walls what will you guys be doing?"

"We'll go golfing," I said. "But, if you prefer, you girls can come along and caddy for us. I think I'd classify that as yard work, too."

16

*I went ice fishing once. All I caught was pneumonia.*
*My buddy, who talked me into this stupid sport,*
*said it would be fun. He lied.*

## SURVIVING WINTER SPORTS

My wife suggested it would be a good idea for us to take up winter sports this year.

"It will keep us physically fit, and help make the winter pass more quickly," she said.

The problem with outdoor sports in the winter is you have to actually do them outdoors, where it's usually cold and snowy.

My idea of a winter sport is drinking hot chocolate by a roaring fire. That's because I've tried winter sports and they're dangerous. All winter sports seem to have been invented by people who believe pain is fun.

For example, I went ice fishing once. All I caught was pneumonia. My buddy, who talked me into this stupid sport, said it would be fun. He lied.

Here is the essence of ice fishing. You punch holes in the ice, put in some bait and stand there, freezing. If you're really dumb, you drink ice cold beer while doing this. More advanced ice fisher-people set up these little houses with stoves, refrigerators, indoor plumbing, jacuzzis and satellite TV reception.

But we were too hearty to do that. "Real ice fisherman take frostbite as a badge of honor," he assured me. I would have answered him sarcastically but a badge of honor had sealed my lips together.

To make a long, very cold story short, we caught four minnows and a smelt that day. I had the smelt mounted and it now hangs on the wall above the fireplace where I drink chocolate in the winter. It's there to remind me never to go ice fishing ever again.

# NO WINTER WIMP

Just so you don't think I'm some kind of wimp who's never done serious outdoor winter sports, I need to tell you I tried bobsledding once. In fact, I had aspirations of becoming an Olympic bobsledder. I figured, "How hard could this sport be? You jump on a sled at the top of a mountain, shift your weight a few times and get out at the bottom to accept your medal."

For those who have never been in a bobsled before, it's basically your average coffin on rails. The essence of the sport, as near as I remember, is to get in the sled and then let gravity take its course. Unfortunately, I never quite got the first step right. All I managed to do was push the sled about 5 feet and slip on the ice. Everybody else jumped in and I waved goodbye to them.

So, it was with some trepidation and a promise we wouldn't be doing any bobsledding or ice fishing, I agreed to try winter sports again with my wife.

To get in shape for this year's winter sports schedule, we had to first go shopping for the right clothes and accessories. Evidently, it's against the rules to do any winter sport unless you've spent at least $500 on equipment you'll use once or twice in a lifetime.

The first sport we equipped ourselves for was cross-country skiing. "It's a great cardiovascular sport, and will only cost about $800 apiece to get you started," the salesman said. The man assured us that if we didn't like cross country-skiing, we could always sell our equipment and clothes at a garage sale next summer and get back $30 or so.

For those who don't know anything about cross-country skiing, it is a Nordic sport, invented by Nordics who have nothing better to do with their time in the winter than ski for hours across the tundra to visit  neighbors. A usual visit goes like this: "Hi Sven. I just spent eight hours skiing across the tundra to get here. Well, got to go home now. Bye."

To do cross-country skiing, you need skis, ski poles and these shoes that make you look like you belong in a circus wearing grease paint and a nose that honks.  Proper cross-country ski attire also includes plenty of layers of absorbent cotton clothes to catch all the sweat your body produces while skiing, so it doesn't roll down your legs and freeze your ankles together.

The first time my wife and I went cross-country skiing, we got about ten feet down the trail and ran into trouble. There was no snow.

"Come on, let's go home and drink hot chocolate by the fire," I said.

Unfortunately, that night it snowed three feet and the next day, the radio announced all major airports and roads were closed, but it was a perfect day for cross-country skiing.

## WOLVES WILL GET YOU

Now, the main objective of cross-country skiing is to keep from falling down and looking stupid. At least that was my objective. I've never really been what you would call coordinated, and the idea of strapping 12-foot skis to my feet and asking me to look graceful in them was a stretch of the imagination.

Within seconds of nailing the skis to my clown shoes, I knew I was in trouble. While other skiers all around me pushed off into the snow-covered woods with an easy modulated gait, I was still trying to figure out how to keep from poking a ski pole into my eye when I fell.

"I've heard that if you fall down in cross-country skis, it's almost impossible to get up," I told my wife, trying to play on her fear of imaginary things I make up. "You're like a turtle that's been turned on its back. You just lie there until you die."

"That is nonsense," she said.

"Oh, yeah. Then, what are all those bodies doing lying beside the trail?" I asked, but she couldn't see them, because they had all been dragged into the forest by wolves.

"Come on, you can do this. It's simple," yelled my wife, Madeline, as she poled figure eights around me. "It's just glide, pole, glide, pole," she cried, looking like some Nordic going to visit a neighbor.

"Maybe you ought to go ski by yourself for a little bit. I'll stay here and practice standing upright for an hour or so," I suggested.

Gliding off down the trail, Madeline made the whole thing look easy.

"Maybe I can do this," I thought. I took a tentative pull on my pole and thrust my right ski over my left ski and promptly fell on my back.

I laid there for a moment with my legs pointing in directions God had never intended them to point, a sharpened pole tip hovering dangerously close to my eye. That's when I decided: "Here is another winter sport I am never going to do again. "

How I managed to get turned over and out of those clown flippers, I have no recollection. The last thing I remember was diving into the back seat of the car as the wolves came rushing out of the woods. Luckily, I escaped unharmed, but the wolves got my skis and poles, for which I am in their debt.

Anyway, we won't be doing cross-country skiing anymore. Next week, we take up falling-downhill skiing. Boy, am I looking forward to that.

*Snow is fun for about two weeks around Christmas time. After*
*that, it becomes a bore like a favorite aunt who comes to*
*your house for a visit and stays 10 weeks and you*
*realize why you don't invite her over more often.*

# SURVIVING THE WINTER BLAHS

We're at the end of January. That's the time of the year when people in northern climates like ours get together and in one communal voice go:

"AAAAAAAAWWWWWWWWWWWWWWW. WON'T WINTER EVER END?

I HATE SNOW. HATE IT. HATE IT. HATE IT. I'M TIRED OF BOOTS AND GLOVES AND WEARING SO MUCH CLOTHES I LOOK LIKE THE GOODYEAR BLIMP WHENEVER I STEP OUTSIDE.

I WANT TO SEE BLUE SKIES AND HEAR BIRDS SING AND GO TO WORK WHEN THE SUN IS SHINING AND ...

OH WHAT'S THE USE? GIVE ME THE SNOW SHOVEL AND I'LL TRY TO FIND OUR FRONT PORCH."

By the way, these are the same people who when you meet them on a beach in Florida during spring break and you ask them how they can take all that snow up north every winter, they go, "I think I'd miss the snow if we I didn't have it."

When you hear them say that, don't believe them.

They've obviously become irrational from standing out in the Florida sun too long waiting in line to get on a ride at Disney World.

The truth is, snow is fun for about two weeks around Christmas time. After that, it becomes a bore like a favorite aunt who comes to your house for a visit and stays 10 weeks and you realize why you don't invite her over more often.

## CHECK YOUR EAR FLAPS

The only time I can remember liking winter was when I was a kid going to elementary school. To prepare for school, our mothers would bundle us up in two sets of pants, leggings, coat, boots, mittens, and a checkered hat with ear flaps. All of this was topped off with a big thick scarf wrapped tightly around your head and eyes, cutting off visibility and the rest of your five senses. On the way to school, you could see packs of kids bundled in winter clothes wandering aimlessly around in circles shouting, "Is there anyone out there who can take my hand and lead me to school?"

At school, it would take us an hour to undress and hang up our winter attire. By then, it was recess and we'd have to get all dressed up again to go outside.

When recess was over, we'd come back in and take an hour to undress, and then was lunch time. After lunch, there was more dressing and undressing for afternoon recess until at last we took our classroom seats at 3 p.m. when the bell would ring for us to go home.

No learning ever occurred in winter because of this. Sometimes, the teachers wouldn't even bother to show up. They'd just put up a cardboard cutout of themselves in front of the class and stay home for weeks at a time.

## SLEEPY, GRUMPY AND DOPEY

Now that I think of it, childhood was probably the last time I enjoyed winter. These days, when winter rolls around, I get cranky and tired and just want to sit inside and drink cocoa and eat potato chips all day.

I thought I was the only one who dealt with winter this way, but scientists have discovered that many people do the same thing. In fact they've learned there's a real illness caused by winter called "Seasonal Affective Disorder," or SAD. This illness is a result of a lack of sunshine in winter and is sometimes called the "Winter Blahs," "Winter Blues" and in some parts of the world "Vacation Time."

What happens is that lack of sunshine in winter causes your body to produce a chemical called Melatonin, which if not killed by sunbeams, attacks your brain and turns you into three of the Seven Dwarfs, i.e. Sleepy, Grumpy and Dopey. I am not making this up.

A group called the National Organization for Seasonal Affective Disorder — NO SAD — estimates there may be 10 million Americans suffering from SAD, while another 25 million are just naturally dopey, grumpy and sleepy.

This illness is more prevalent in northern areas, where it is cold and snowy and dark most of the time, places like Michigan. Another place where SAD finds many victims is Sweden. Some parts of Sweden only get a few hours of sunlight a day in winter, which many believe leads to Ingmar Bergman movies where everyone walks around being miserable, then they die. Another side effect of this kind of severe light deprivation is you start to talk Swedish.

One way of treating SAD is by staying outside a lot and exercising, although I've tried this treatment and all it did was give me the sniffles and frost bite.

A more popular treatment of SAD, according to physicians, is *light* therapy where you sit under sun lamps for 15 minutes each day. Taking a southern vacation in winter can also do the trick. Getting sunlight on your body produces a happy hormone called Serotonin, or Ninotores spelled backward, which turns on the part of the brain that tells us to be happy again. This remedy works especially well if you're getting your sunlight on a beach in Florida, which is where I'm headed right now before I start talking Swedish.

So Bjorn Borge to you all.

# Chapter 2
# SURVIVING MODERN LIFE

*What a world we live in today. Cars disintegrate on impact, but I need a sledge hammer to open CD cases. We don't know our neighbors but can call anyone, any place in the world. Self-help books tell us what we're doing wrong, but most of it is caused by heredity. If we wanted, we could change this world, but who has the time?*

*I've chipped teeth trying to bite open airline pretzel packs.*
*And, around our place, we now use jars of pickles*
*as home decorations because we*
*can't get at the contents.*

# SURVIVING EASY-OPEN PACKAGING

I have a modern dilemma that has been vexing me for quite some time.

The issue is this. Why can a four-year-old child crumple the bumper of my car with a hefty kick, but I need the jaws of life to pry open a bag of peanuts?

Something is wrong in the world when the clear plastic container on a Barbi Doll is virtually indestructible, but the tires on a SUV fall apart from hitting pebbles in the road.

It's beginning to look like the auto industry should start hiring product package designers to create more durable cars, while auto engineers could fill jobs to create easy-open cereal bags that come apart with a single pull without a person having to have the strength of Charles Atlas to open the bag.

The other day while having breakfast I tried to open a cellophane bag of corn flakes and I nearly got a hernia while struggling to pull the 1/100th inch of sealed paper apart. I finally had to stab the packaging with a Ginsu knife to get it open. I wonder if NASA is aware of the secrets of corn flakes packaging. They could build space shuttles out of the stuff.

I think we've all had to wrestle with the problem of containers and packaging that won't open. I gave up long ago on safety sealed jars of spaghetti sauce that won't open no matter if you twist the lid until your face turns red and your eyes pop out. I've chipped teeth trying to bite open airline pretzel packs. And, around our place, we now use jars of pickles as home decorations because we can't get at the contents.

This is a serious national problem because as the babyboom generation ages and gets weaker, the containers of "iron pill" supplements and "Lean Cuisine" we need to sustain life keep getting harder to open. I fully expect some day to come across a story in the newspaper about an elderly gentleman who is found starved to death trying to pry off the cellophane seal on a jar of mayonnaise.

## PLEASE BITE HERE

Not only is product packaging getting harder to open, it's also getting trickier. Our family has had a plastic bottle of ketchup in a our refrigerator for two years and it's still full. No one figured out you had to take the lid off and unplug the safety seal inside to use it.

We just kept bringing home those small packages of McDonald's ketchup for our sandwiches, which themselves are next to impossible to open, except when you leave them on the seat of your car. Then, they open all by themselves.

McDonald's ketchup packages have a cut at the top with the words "open here" on them. One would think you could just rip these little puppies apart with your hands. But no, I always have to bite them to get them open. They should put little teeth marks on the ketchup pack where you're supposed to open them with the words "bite here."

Actually the most frustrating packaging to open is the wrappings on video tapes and CDs. The packaging material is airtight and laminated to the case like they are sealing a time capsule to last into the next century. You can't pull it apart with your hands. You can't cut it with your fingernails. You can't even bite into the packaging. And every time I use my Ginsu knife to slice into the protective packaging I cut myself. The last time I almost gouged an eye out.

In fact, CD packages are so hard to open the industry calls them "jewel cases" because you need to be a safe cracker to get into them. To solve the problem of opening CDs I went on the Internet, which has answers to every known problem, and I turned up an article on how to open a CD pack in 14 easy steps. The directions went like this:

## HOW TO OPEN A CD CASE
WARNING: DO NOT TRY TO OPEN CD CASE WITH GINSU KNIFE OR OTHER SHARP OBJECTS AS YOU MIGHT GOUGE YOUR EYE OUT.

DIRECTIONS:

1. Holding the case parallel to the floor, grasp upper right-hand corner firmly between thumb and forefinger.
2. Insert thumbnail of non-holding hand under folded transparent shrink-wrap located at corner of bottom edge of CD case.
3. Gently pry upper layer of shrink-wrap with fingernail and begin prying loose the shrink-wrap.
4. Keep prying loose the shrink wrap.
5. Continue to keep prying loose the shrink wrap.
6. If this fails, bite corner of shrink wrap near teeth mark and rip off all shrink-wrap covering by any and all means possible.

I tried those directions and after ten minutes I finally succeed in getting the protective shrink wrap off, but then I still had the daunting challenge of opening the jewel case itself. Here are the directions to open the case.

7. Lay case on flat surface with hinged area pointing toward your body.
8. Hold case firmly on flat surface with left hand.
9. Use right hand to raise large heavy object such as a sledge hammer over your head.
10. Bring sledge hammer in contact with jewel case with powerful downward motion, being careful not to smash fingers of left hand.

Success. Your CD is open and ready to play.

Now, if someone would please loan me their "jaws of life," I could open my airline pretzels and enjoy the music.

*I was surprised by the complexity of my new cellular phone. It has 43 keys and buttons that will allow me to do any number of things with it, including interplanetary messages and teleporting small animals short distances.*

# SURVIVING THE CELL PHONE

I finally broke down and got a cellular phone.

After years of resisting the temptation to be able to talk with someone while doing my grocery shopping or speeding down the highway, I now have the capacity to call anyone, anytime from anywhere.

My children where duly impressed.

"Dad," they cried in unison. "You've finally made it."

I have to admit, I have been a little slow in embracing the technological wonders of mass communications of the 21st century. In fact, it was only recently that I came to grips with cordless telephones, let alone the concept of digital cellular long-distance communication.

You see, I come from a different era. When I was growing up 50 years ago, a telephone was a device that sat in your living room or kitchen and rang when you had a call. Phones didn't go cruising around the country in your shirt pocket or purse. A telephone knew its place in those days, and stayed at home.

### DIFFERENT PHONE WORLD

It was a different world of phone communications back in that era than today.

When I went to pick out my new phone recently, I found I had dozens of phones and companies to choose from. Back in the 1950s, there was only one telephone company, which looked after all of your communication needs. That company was called "Ma Bell," and it had one style of phone, which was black and made out of steel that had been recycled from World War II battleships.

Unlike today's snazzy three-ounce cellular phones that you can slip into your pocket and take anywhere, our home phone weighed about 20 pounds and was attached to the house by a long black cord. You could only carry the phone as far as the line would stretch. Then you stopped.

I can remember reading about people whose lives were spared when they fell out of second story windows holding the phone and were saved by the phone line. Just try that with a cellular phone.

In those days, we rented our telephone for 50 cents a month from the phone company. I have no idea whether I rent or own this phone. All I know is I took out insurance on it. If it disappears or falls into a toilet, I get another one.

## BEAM ME UP, SCOTTY

With my new phone I also got 5 million free minutes, where I can call anywhere in the country. Calling long distance has become so common that no one thinks anything of it, but I still remember when it was a major event to call someone long distance.

Once, back in 1955, we called my father's uncle, Mike, long distance in Detroit. It took us a month to plan the call. We even sent him a letter to tell him what time and day we would be calling and what we were going to say. When we finally made the call we spent all of our time shouting, "Can you hear us, uncle? We can hear you." That was our entire three-minute conversation.

I was surprised by the complexity of my new cellular phone. It has 43 keys and buttons that will allow me to do any number of things with it, including interplanetary messages and teleporting small animals short distances. In contrast, my family's first telephone didn't even have a dial. You picked up the receiver and a voice of the operator on the other end said, "Number, please?" And you responded with, "Give me Plaza 555." I always thought having your own personal telephone operator to do your bidding was kind of classy.

Now, compare that to today's technology and what have you got? I made a phone call the other day to a local company and got an electronic voice that told me to punch in my party's extension, or, if I didn't know the extension, to type in their name using the telephone keypad.

Have you ever tried to spell out Marvin Wirshwitkowski on a telephone keypad? It's not easy, I'll tell you. After I spent about 20 minutes figuring out the various numbers, I got almost to the "ski" part when the automatic phone hung up on me. Give me a real live operator any day.

## PARTY LINE LISTENING

Today, the big issue with cellular phones is security and privacy. We didn't have to worry about that back in the 1950s. We had none. We were all on a party line, which meant we shared the telephone line with three other people somewhere in our town.

Each of us had our own special ring. Our phone would ring one long and two short rings to let us know we had a call coming in. Two long and one short ring belonged to someone else on the line, and one long, one short and one long was for the third party.

The different phone rings told you when your household had a call coming in so the other parties wouldn't pick up. Of course, all of us picked up the phone whenever it rang and listened in anyway. That's how we knew what was going on in town. Of course, you can listen in on cell phone conversations today, but it costs you extra.

As I said, my kids were quite pleased with my new telephone, and wanted to know all about.

"Does your cell phone have call waiting?" asked Matt.

"Can you do e-mail with it? "asked my son, Nathan.

"Can you order pizza on it?" asked my son, Jason.

I could only tell them the truth.

"I don't know," I said. "I haven't figured out how to turn it on yet."

*While most people slam the phone down on telemarketers, I have found over the years that talking with these people can be more enjoyable than disco dancing.*

# SURVIVING TELEMARKETERS

I don't know what you like to do with your free time, but whenever I have a spare afternoon or evening I like to sit around and talk with telemarketing sales people on the telephone.

I know most people find telemarketers annoying and an intrusion on their lives, but I'll tell you, if you have the time to talk with them, they can be loads of fun. While most people slam the phone down on telemarketers, I have found over the years that talking with these people can be more enjoyable than disco dancing.

You have to realize these people sit for hours each day, getting minimum wage, reading prepared scripts about the benefits of high interest credit cards, storm door replacements and holistic preventions against "Mad Cow" disease with hardly anyone providing variety in their poor dull lives except the occasional "No thank you" before someone slams the phone in their ear.

A while back I started playing games with these people in my alter ego "The Telemarketing Terminator" where I would require telemarketing people to solve riddles, name the capitals of North and South Dakota or sing me the Star Spangled Banner before I would let them talk with me. Surprisingly, most of them went along with my requests because they are not financing their way through college in these jobs.

I have become more sophisticated over time and now I try to create personalities on my end of the phone line that have a problem with whatever the telemarketer is selling me. Here's a synopsis of three recent phone calls I received last week. Although the names have been changed to protect the innocent, these are all true calls and you can do them yourself with a little imagination and a lot of free time.

# CREDIT CARD OFFERS

**Marketer:** Hi, I'm Sarah with Charge-It-To-The-Max credit card company and I'm happy to inform you Mr. Kuckley, you have been pre-approved for our card to a maximum of $100,000.

**Me:** (scared voice) Oh, thank God you called, I've just been sitting here wondering how to pay off all those gambling debts I owe before someone kills me.

**Marketer:** Yes, you can pay off all your other high interest cards with the Charge-It-To-The-Max credit card and have only one easy monthly payment.

**Me:** Will this cover money I owe to loan sharks, too?

**Marketer:** You can use the money for most credit card debts and your transfers will be charged a small annual percentage fee of only 9.5 percent for the first..."

**Me:** How about if I promise to pay 100 percent interest. Can I get $50,000 right now if I promise not to pay it back for a year?

**Marketer:** Why would you want to do that?

**Me:** Well, if I borrowed $50,000 tomorrow and didn't pay it back, I'd owe you $100,000 at the end of the year; and if I used another $50,000 the next year and didn't pay anything for that year, I'd owe you about $300,000 with compounded interest. Your company would be way ahead and happy.

**Marketer:** You have to pay something. Like if you buy a $50 pair of shoes you have to pay the credit card company $50.

**Me:** How many times? The guy I borrow from now makes me pay $100 a week on a $1,000 loan and won't tell me when I'm done. Does your company do that?

**Marketer:** No, you get a monthly statement that shows....

**Me:** What about if I'm late with my payments? Does your firm send out someone to break my legs if I'm late paying?

**Marketer:** I don't believe so.  We do have a service fee for late payments.

**Me:** That's a relief.  Hey, send me the card right away. And can you put it in the name of John Smith?

## LAW ENFORCEMENT

**Marketer:**  "Hi, I'm representing the State Police Benevolent Society and we're seeking donation to help make your community safer.

**Me:**  (Rough sounding voice) Hey, I donate directly.

**Marketer:** How is that sir?

**Me:** You know bribes, Christmas gifts. Under the table stuff.

**Marketer:**  Ah…your donation will go to a statewide organization that...

**Me:** Don't you guys ever quit with the shakedowns. Just because my business partner disappeared after taking out a big company loan that is now unaccounted for, why do you have to keep bothering me?
I mean every time a body part shows up, I got a cop on my door asking, "Do you know anything about this leg we just found?" and I got to give him some donation to go away. I mean it's breaking me, man.

**Marketer:**  I don't know anything about that sir. The reason I'm calling is..."

**Me:** Yeah, well you ain't going to get any more money unless you start helping me.

**Marketer:** I don't understand. I'm calling on behalf of ...

**Me:** Here's the deal. I got this nosey neighbor who thinks I buried something in her garden and she keeps giving me the fish eye and calling the cops on me. I'd like one of your people to pay a visit to her ... you know convince her it would be in the best interest of her health to move to Arizona or somewhere. Then you might get a donation.

**Marketer:** I don't believe our organization could do anything like that even for a donation.

**Me:** Then what good are you?

### WINDOW REPLACEMENTS

**Marketer:** Hi, sir, I'm Jane Story and I would like to talk with you about new storm windows.

**Me:** (shouting) IS THIS 911?

**Marketer:** No, this is Jane at Ever-seal windows and...

**Me:** My God, lady, call 911 for me.

**Marketer:** I don't believe I'm in your calling area.

**Me:** Lady, I've cut off the fingers on both my hands in a freak Ginsu knife accident. Please call 911 for me. I'm bleeding all over the place.

**Marketer:** Sir, my manual doesn't cover that. Can't you dial 911 yourself?

**Me:** Look, I don't have any fingers and I'm holding the phone up to my ear with my foot.

**Marketer:** I'm sorry sir, I'll have to call you back at a more convenient time.

*There should be some kind of special punishment for people who play their music so loud that it sets your feet a-tapping even if your feet are stuck in hardened cement.*

# SURVIVING LOUD MUSIC

I was stopped at a traffic light the other day when a car pulled up beside me with its radio on. I could tell the radio was on in the other car because I could hear it in my car with the windows rolled up and my hands over my ears.

Every time the music hit a bass note, which was every beat, my car would shudder and the little fuzzy dice on my rear-view mirror would bounce. I looked over at the car, which was slightly larger than the size of the speakers in the back seat, and shook my head. I didn't intend to shake my head, it was really an involuntary muscle spasm produced by the noise.

The driver of the car was totally oblivious to the noise he was making, even when the sound waves knocked down an elderly couple who were crossing the street in front of us. I looked over at the driver. He had blood trickling out of his ears.

I think there should be some kind of special punishment for people who play their music so loud that it sets your feet a-tapping even if your feet are stuck in hardened cement.

Well, the little town of Fort Lupton, Colo., has come up with a unique way to punish people who play their car and home noise machines way too loud. The courts there sentence offenders caught with their radio blasting, to listen to several hours of bagpipe music. Now, I don't want to go offending bagpipe music lovers. Bagpipe music does have its place. For instance, they're great in parades and, of course, as punishment for people who play their stereos too loud.

The Fort Lupton police, who host mandatory monthly concerts for those convicted of having speaker systems that are worth more than the car they're driving, also like to mix up their musical punishment with selections like the "Barney" theme song and orchestral arrangements of "Moonlight Sonata."

## CRIME AND PUNISHMENT

I thought, "Now, here is a perfect example of the punishment fitting the crime." I thought that until I read the rest of the songs on the police play list. Included in their musical punishment category was Wayne Newton's "Danke Schoen." Hey, I like that song. I used to get to hold hands and roller skate with girls when that song came on at the rink. What are these people in Fort Lupton trying to say? That I have bad taste in music.

That wasn't the worst of it. The police hit list also included Beethoven's Fifth Symphony, which goes, "Dah, dah, dah, da. Dah, dah, dah, da," "Happy Trails to You" by Roy Rogers and Dale Evans, and Hugo Montenegro's "The Good, the Bad and the Ugly" that goes "Da, da, da, da, dah, da, da, dah."

I love those songs. I've got memories invested in that music. I can remember dressing up in my little cowboy outfit with the fringed vest, white hat and six-gun and singing along with Roy and Dale as their little red record spun on the old RCA Victrola. I used to do the same thing to Hugo Montenegro's "The Good, the Bad, and the Ugly."

Why did they pick these songs? I can think of hundreds of songs they could play that wouldn't offend anyone's musical taste such as, "Disco Duck." Go ahead, I dare anyone out there to tell me they think "Disco Duck" is a fine piece of music.

## PUT YOUR BACK SIDE IN

They could also play the "Piña Colada" song, "Simon Says" by the 1910 Fruit Gum Co., "Does your chewing gum lose its flavor on the bedpost overnight?" and anything by the guy from "Baywatch." I'd also throw in a few crowd-pleasing wedding songs, like the "Hokey Pokey" and the "Macarena."

Don't get me wrong, I used to enjoy the "Hokey Pokey" when I was 10 years old. When I hear that song now, I'm always reminded of how the other kids and I used to stand along the dance floor and laugh when the old folk put their back sides in to "shake them all about." As for the "Macarena," it brings back bad memories of a Christmas we got a singing gorilla. It sang that song non-stop for the 12 days of Christmas and then some.

I'm sure you can add your own list of least-loved songs to this group. Some people already have suggested "Me and Mrs. Jones," "Teen Angel," "Polka Your Eyes Out," and "Boys will be Boys" be included in the Fort Lupton court-sponsored "sock hop."

I was going to suggest that the police also include some Rap music in their top ten punishers, but then I realized that would be defeating the whole point of the punishment. Besides, complaining about new music would also make me sound like my mother when she'd yell at me for playing "The Good, the Bad and the Ugly." She'd go, "Why do you have to play that noise so loud?" And I'd answer, "Mom, I'm 50 years old. It's my house and it's not noise."

*I've got to believe if life were simple, they'd just give you a
one-page Xerox instruction sheet on how to live when
you're born and then send you yearly
updates on the Internet.*

# SURVIVING SELF-HELP BOOKS

I was complaining the other day about how things never seem to go the way I want them to, when one of my friends popped in with some advice. He said, "If life gives you lemons, just make lemonade."

I said I was an iced tea drinker myself, but I knew what he meant. Make the best of what you've got. Only that doesn't work for me. If I tried to make lemonade out of my problems, I'd just get juice in my eye, cut my finger because I couldn't see and then bleed all over my shirt.

That's what's wrong with instant advice. It's easy to give, hard to do, and half the time it gets you into more trouble than if you'd just left the stupid lemons sitting on the counter in a nice bowl, arranged with some other fresh fruits as a decoration.

As you can probably guess, I don't subscribe to instant "life fixes" that will solve all your problems if you just do this, that or make lemonade. Yet, everywhere I turn these days, there are self-help articles and books on how to fix your messed-up love life, failing career, childhood or bathroom faucet in seven easy steps.

All you've got to do is plunk down $25 — hey, fixing your messed-up life doesn't come cheap these days — read the book, and you'll be fast on your way to a more enjoyable and fruitful life.

I've got to believe if life were so simple, they'd just give you a one-page Xerox instruction sheet on how to live when you're born and then send you yearly updates on the Internet, i.e. "It's now time to fix your life with these seven easy steps ...."

# INSTANT SELF-HELP

Self-help books seem to have five things in common. One, the author is an expert on something, and two, the book has a nifty "catch" phrase that sums up the entire philosophy of the book in four words. (I realize that's only two things these books have in common, but I said there were five things because I have a problem with exaggeration. But, I'm working on it. So just leave me alone. OK?)

A trip to your local book store turns up hundreds of intriguing titles, with advice for everything that ails you. Here's just a short list I recently compiled of some of the more intriguing self-help books.

> *"Nine Steps to Instant Success, You Loser."*
> *"The Book for Everything That Ails You."*
> *"Feeling Good About Feeling Bad."*
> *"The Cigar Diet."*
> *"Think Thin and Win"*
> *"Do-it-Yourself Liposuction."*
> *"Polka Yourself to Good Health."*
> *"Cabbage Soup for the Soul."*

In one store alone, I found more than 100 books for women on how to find the right man. On the next row were 200 books on how to get rid of the wrong guy and find true happiness with chocolate.

Self-help books on marriage are also popular. One called "Guide to a Perfect Marriage" was 480 pages of the words, "Yes, dear." One shelf down was a book titled "Everything Men Know About Women." It was a quick read. All the pages were blank.

Some of the titles on personal improvement attracted me. One book that caught my eye was titled "Overcoming Indecision." I stood there for three hours going, "Should I buy it? Or shouldn't I buy it? Do I need it? No. But, maybe I do."

Another book I thought I could use was called, "Putting off Procrastination," but I decided to get it later.

## IT'S FULGHUM'S FAULT

Actually, I blame author Robert Fulghum for starting all this stuff with his book "All I Really Need to Know I Learned in Kindergarten." It's a simple credo of sharing things, playing fair and not hitting people. All I ever learned in kindergarten was to keep my head down during nap time or else Sister Superior would hit me with a yardstick. I was the school's best napper by first grade.

When I was a kid we didn't have all these instant advice gurus. The only magazine that offered regular "How-to" articles was Popular Mechanics, which featured articles on building brick barbecue grills in your back yard. I grew up thinking that all I needed to have for a good life, perfect marriage and afternoons of fun in the sun was a brick grill and rotisserie with warming oven. See how deceiving these articles can be.

Other than Popular Mechanics articles, we had to depend on old-fashioned "folk wisdom" to get us through.

People would say, "Rome wasn't built in a day" whenever you had to wait for something you wanted. Or, they'd tell you, "a bird in the hand is worth two in the bush," to mean you should be happy with what you had.

The one I could never figure out was "don't cut your nose off to spite your face." I'd come home from school and my mother would call out to me "get washed up for dinner, and don't cut your nose off to spite your face." I figure there was probably a lot of nose slicing going on back then by people trying to make lemonade.

There was one bit of wisdom, though, that I've carried with me through the years. I'm not sure who wrote it, but it goes something like this. "A person is a success who has lived well, laughed often and loved much and who leaves the world a better place than they found it."

*One does have to wonder why for the $27 overdraft charge,
banks couldn't call you up immediately and say, "Hey,
dummy you got no cash at the bank and you're
bouncing checks all over the place."*

## SURVIVING BANK SERVICES

I love the banking industry.  Everyone in banking is so friendly and helpful that I just want to reach into my back pocket and make sure my wallet is still there every time I deal with one of our nation's great financial institutions.

For the past few weeks I've been having a wonderful experience working with a new banking company I'll call the Third Fourth Amalgamated Bank of Idaho. Third Fourth Bank recently purchased a 100 year old local bank where I kept part of my retirement nest egg — about $16.

The money sat in a checking account for a couple years. I probably should have closed the account a long time ago, but it didn't seem to be hurting anyone and I felt good knowing I had a little money stashed away in case I had to pay for lunch or an oil change some day.

Anyway, my little checking account had gone through a secession of banking mergers over the years, all of whom let my cash sit there unmolested until Third Fourth Second Bank of Idaho and Denver took over.  Whether through my inattention, or that mythical creature — banking error — I got a notice from the good people at the bank that I was $1.16 overdrawn.

For being overdrawn 116 cents I got hit with a "Not Enough Funds" charge of $27, or the equivalent of 2,327.58 percent weekly interest on my $1.16 indiscretion.  Of course the bank, which does everything instantaneously and electronically, sent me notice of my grievous error via Carrier Pigeon from their main office in Potato Field, Idaho. My notice arrived promptly at my doorstep in seven days — which is not bad arrival time considering Carrier Pigeons have been extinct for nearly a century.

By the time I opened the statement that let me know I was overdrawn, I owed the bank an extra $35 daily inattention fees — $5 per day penalty for every day my friendly bank overdraft notice wandered its way cross-country to me.

So with the $35 on top of the $27 fee, I now owed a total of $62, or, according to my calculations, approximately 5,344.8 percent interest on my $1.16 overdraft for ten days. I thought this was a bit excessive. Just think if I had been out of the country for a month and didn't find my notices for 30 days, I would owe them approximately $177, or 15,258.6 percent interest on my $1.16 overdraft.

## PROCEDURAL OVERSIGHT

I don't want to leave the impression that I'm picking on the Third Fourth Second Seventh Amalgamated Bank of Denver and Idaho. From my experience with other banks, they all do these charges the same way. In other words, they charge you $27 for overdrafts, notify you by Pony Express — which has been out of service for 130 years — and happily keep collecting more fees until you open your week-old mail and discover you've bounced another dozen checks in the interim.

I'm sure this is just a procedural oversight on the part of the banking industry. I would never suggest that banks that can do ten million transactions in the blink of an eye with their computers would intentionally make notification of overdrafts an extremely slow process so they can make lots more money off your initial mistake.

One does have to wonder why for the $27 overdraft charge, banks couldn't have an automated phone system to call you up immediately on the first overdraft that says, "Hey, dummy you got no cash at the bank and you're bouncing checks all over the place." People in banking have told me this would be a very complicated and expensive system, just like the very expensive complicated automated callback systems banks use to notify you that you owe them mucho casho two weeks after you're in the hole to them.

I'm sure banks would put in a quick overdraft notification system if it weren't so darn complex that it has to be the only thing in the entire banking industry handled by bulk mail. I really don't think it has anything to do with the fact that if 1 million checks get bounced daily, banks make $27 million for one day on Non Sufficient Funds charges. The fact that this translates out to about $20 billion a year in revenue for the industry also probably doesn't influence their decision to use snail mail for overdraft notification. I'd never suggest that.

Anyway, after a half-dozen phone calls to my newly merged bank, the Fifth Third Sixth Second and a Half Bank of Wyoming and Cleveland and its automated customer service system, I managed to find out exactly nothing from them about what occurred to my $16 account except the bank needed more fees, more often, from me. So, I decided to pay them a personal visit.

## FRIENDLY LOAN SHARK

Outside the bank, though, I ran into this shady looking character in a pin-striped suit and sunglasses sitting at a folding table. His name was Freddie the Friendly Loan Shark.

"Hey buddy," he said, capturing my attention with a rolled up racing form. "I can tell by the hangdog look on your face that you are an individual with banking problems. Probably, in the specific area of overdraft fees."

"Wow," I said. "Are you psychic or something?"

"No, I'm just a student of human nature and the international banking system," he said with some modesty. "My guess is you just got hit with some outrageous bank fees for coming up a few clams short of a dozen in your account."

"Yeah, that's exactly what happened," I said.

"Well, your problems are over, buddy. Just open a checking account with me and you'll never have to worry about outrageous bank fees again," he said.

"Here's how I work. You put your money with me, Freddie the Friendly Loan Shark Nearly Legitimate Bank, and then write as many monthly checks against it as you want. You go over

44

what you got with FFLNLB and I charge you $50, no questions asked," he explained.

"Well, $50 sounds a little high considering my bank charges only $27 for an overdraft," I said.

"But we only charge you once," explained Freddie. "Then, we call you up. You come pay your fifty bucks. And we're square."

"And if I don't pay?" I asked.

"We send over our Customer Service Representative, 'Bubba,' who breaks your leg," he said.

"That sounds a lot worse than bank fees," I said.

"The big service is this. We break your leg once," he explained. "We don't notify you by Viking Warrior ship that your account is overdrawn and then keep breaking your leg until your notice arrives."

"I can see where that would be a plus," I said, knowing that a single notice from 'Bubba' would prompt immediate payment of the debt.

"With us, you get quick notice, and you fix the problem for a small onetime fee. Everybody's happy, including your leg," he said.

I hate to say it, but my $1.16 problem is solved. 'Bubba' had a talk with the bank. It was just one of the many services provided by Freddie the Friendly Loan Shark Nearly Legal Bank, who now gets all my business.

*Our sons would spend hours each evening playing "Donkey Kong" and "Centipede" on their Nintendo game, their childhoods and adolescence lost to smashing electronic snails with a wooden mallet.*

# SURVIVING SILICON VALLEY STUFF

Anthropologists on the West Coast are studying the artifacts, culture and tribal history of the Silicon Man.

No, this is not some long-lost civilization that lived in California before it was trendy. The researchers are digging into the everyday lives of people who live in Silicon Valley, the epicenter of technological development in the United States.

Silicon Valley, if you don't know it, is the birthplace of the electronic adding machine, the first video game, the personal computer, the digital bathroom scale and thousands of other electronic devices that become obsolete the day after I buy them.

The Valley is also the birthplace of the 100-hour work week, the idea of 24/7 (operating 24 hours a day, seven days a week) and the motto "Thank God it's Friday. There's only two more workdays 'til Monday."

According to researchers, people in Silicone Valley spend all of their waking hours creating and using electronic gizmos like the "Palm Pilot," a $300 personal organizer that replaces a $3 desk calendar.

The anthropologists have spent nine years researching the effects of super high-tech lives on people and their families. So far, they've discovered that these timesaving, labor-saving electronic devices use up more time and create more work than they save. I could have told them that.

## LIFE WAS GOOD

Twenty years ago, before the electronics/communications revolution, my life was good. It basically revolved around getting up in the morning, going to work for eight hours, coming home, playing with the kids, having dinner and falling asleep to reruns of "Gilligan's Island."

On weekends, I'd make fancy omelet breakfasts for the family, wash the car, do some chores around the house and maybe take everyone out for a movie in the evening. In summer, we'd go to the beach and watch the sun set as the kids splashed in the water.

Then, the computer arrived. At work, I went from dashing off two-minute, handwritten memos a department secretary would type into intelligible, grammatically correct English, to spending hours laboriously pecking out my own scribbled missives on my desktop computer.

And it never failed, when I was done, the computer would promptly make all my work disappear when I hit the print button. I figure computers added 20 hours a week to my job.

Then came electronic mail, the most insidious of all electronic time wasters. Suddenly people in all parts of the company, who I didn't even know, could send me e-mails on subjects I had no interest in, didn't apply to my job, but required a reply.

I found myself writing more e-mail letters in a single day than all the letters I sent to my parents in four years of college.

At home, video games replaced "Gilligan's Island" on the TV. Our sons would spend hours each evening playing "Donkey Kong" and "Centipede" on their Nintendo game, their childhoods and adolescence lost to smashing electronic snails with a wooden mallet.

Today, when our boys get together to talk over old times, they say things like, "Remember game 3,487 of "Space Invaders" when I scored 67,459,948 points and you only got 59,553,421?"

My kids still believe Lara Croft is a real person. One of the boys invited her to his school's homecoming dance.

# THE VCR DOWNFALL

My electronic downfall wasn't video games, but the VCR. I was an avid TV watcher in my younger days before the VCR, but after its invention I took to staying up to 4 a.m. each night watching television programs I had taped while watching other shows. Go ahead ask me any question about Alex and Valerie Keaton on "Family Ties." The only thing I can't tell you is why Alex Keaton changed his name when he moved to New York to work for the mayor on "Spin City."

To make matters worse, former Vice President Al Gore had to go out and invent the Internet so I could get tons of e-mail advertisements on my computer, offering to sell me phony doctorate degrees in any major I want, (i.e. "Ethics,") or show me how to discover secret information on anyone. (I wonder if these two companies are working in conjunction with each other?)

Now, with the internet, I spend hours each day deleting messages from people in different parts of the world I don't even know, who send me e-mail messages on subjects I have no interest in, and don't apply to my life. Worse yet, I get dozens of messages every day from friends and colleagues who believe forwarding e-mail jokes is some form of communication.

And on top of it all, I have to spend time downloading anti- virus software to protect my computer files from nasty things people attach to e-mail jokes they send to my friends that get passed on to me.

So, I have no sympathy for the Silicon Valley tribe and their 100-hour work weeks, where kids carry pictures of Bill Gates in their wallets instead of rock stars, and parents are so busy they think spending quality time with their children is talking to them on cell phones.

If these people really want to invent an electronic device that will save us all time and work, then they should invent a digital time machine so we can all go back 20 years to sit in front of our television sets watching reruns of "Gilligan's Island."

# Chapter 3
# SURVIVING THE GREAT OUTDOORS

*Nature looks beautiful but it's all an illusion. The world outside is full of nasty things like killer bees, conniving squirrels and lawn and garden experts. There are also other dangers such as deck building and deer hunting that can befall you. The safest place to survive the outdoors is from inside your home. That's why screen doors and windows were invented.*

*It's not like I don't have enough things in the world to worry about that can bite, claw and inject me with poisonous venom. Now, I've got to worry about Killer Bees coming into my home.*

## SURVIVING KILLER BEES

There's only one thing over the years that has kept me from giving up on Michigan and its cold, snowy winters and moving south to warmer climates. That's the thought of living with Killer Bees.

Killer Bees don't like cold weather. Therefore, Michigan winters — which usually last from October to sometime in the middle of June — are my only defense against Killer Bees; that African bully bee, with a quick temper that has nothing better to do than sting people.

I've been tracking the progress of Killer Bees since the late 1950s, when some lunatic scientist decided to import these nasty things from Africa to South America so we could have our own strain of Killer Bees in this hemisphere.

At first I hoped, like many other sane people, that the Gulf of Mexico and U.S. Immigration would prevent the Killer Bees from moving to this country. But since the 1960s, they've been making their way northward, stopped so far only by the snow barrier. I constantly worry that El Niño, which brought us a mild winter and early spring this year, will change our weather patterns and make it warm and hospitable for the Killer Bees where I live.

### ONCE BITTEN, TWICE AFRAID

It's not like I don't have enough things in the world to worry about that can bite, claw and inject me with poisonous venom. Now, I've got to worry about Killer Bees coming into my home along with vampire bats, sea nettles and Black Widow spiders. Put that on top of your homegrown variety of stinging wasps, bumble bees and yellow jackets, and the insidious Brown Recluse Spider, and my plate is full.

You see, I have this totally rational fear of stinging things. I've been a bee worrier since I was a little kid. It all started when I got stung once when I was 5 years old and stepped on a bee in some clover. All I can say is, it's a good thing it wasn't a Killer Bee, or I wouldn't be around today to write about it.

But it was a catastrophic event in my childhood. My little baby toe swelled up to size of my big toe, and it hurt.  It took my parents years to get me over that painful experience and convince me that it was OK to go out of the house without mosquito netting draped over my entire body.

## THE "DANCE OF LIFE"

As I grew into a teenager, and it became harder to find girls who would go out with someone wearing beekeeper apparel, I abandoned the protective outerwear and instead took up a more mature response to stinging insects. I developed the "dance of life."

The "dance of life" is a simple defensive maneuver I practice whenever anything buzzing comes within 10 feet of me. To do the dance, I simply start slapping my hands on my head and body while jumping around erratically in circles. To this sequence, I usually add short dashes across the yard where I stop and pause before thrashing around some more.

When people see me do this at family gatherings, picnics or on downtown streets in summer, they often think, "Well, this has been fun, but we have to go now."

Silly as my little "dance of life" sounds, I've never been stung by a bee while doing it. My theory is, if you move fast enough, the stinging thing attacking you can't zero in on an artery or tender, defenseless earlobe. The other theory of why I don't get stung during the dance — a theory which is held by my family and friends — is that I scare off the poor insect because I'm acting like a crazy man.

The truth is, the "dance of life" is only successful if it is accompanied by placing my tongue on the roof of my mouth while doing it. Sometimes (like if I'm in at a luncheon for the Princess of the Netherlands and don't want to people to think I'm insane by doing the "dance of life" on a table top) I can just put my tongue on the roof of my mouth and be protected. This only works indoors. Outside, you still have to do the "dance of life" or you get stung.

Over the years, people have repeatedly told me not to pay attention to these flying stinging things. "Just ignore them and they'll go away," they say. These are usually the same people who are deathly afraid of things like caterpillars, which can neither fly nor sting, and couldn't catch up with me in a 10-yard dash in a week or more. The worst a caterpillar can do is crawl up your pant leg with a bunch of other caterpillars and give you a slow, but painful, wedgie. I know that from experience.

## ACTING LIKE A MANIAC

There are only two times in my whole life when I've resisted acting like a total maniac around stinging insects (actually three if you count the luncheon with the Princess). One was when my son, Nathan, and I were walking in the woods and this giant, eagle-size bumble bee came and landed on his back. In a moment of unselfish, fatherly love—and without thought to the horrendous danger to my own self—I reached over and brushed it off and chased it away.

The other occasion was my wedding day.

As my blushing bride and I stood at the altar before the congregation, ready to exchange our vows, a honey bee appeared from among the flowers and began circling over our heads. Not wanting to embarrass my future wife by doing the "dance of life" before our families and 200 close friends, I stood my ground clamping my tongue firmly to the roof of my mouth. As I watched the bee fly around my head, I heard those faithful words, "Do you take this woman to be your wife," and with my tongue on the roof of my mouth, I responded with all my heart, "I doodth."

*In two decades of burying thousands of pounds of seeds, potato eyes, broccoli stems and other defenseless root plants in the ground, I've only produced a garden once that would make Martha Stewart proud of me.*

# SURVIVING THE PERFECT GARDEN

It's the end of July and, as I write this, I look out over the garden outside my kitchen window and wonder in amazement at the crop of fresh vegetables springing from the black earth in neat well-tended rows. There's not a weed in sight, not a blemish or aphid on a single plant.

I take great pride in that garden, often bringing friends and associates over to look out the window to marvel at what is by any standards a class "A," number one vegetable patch.

Of course, I never take them outside the house to look at it. If I did, they'd discover the garden is really in my neighbor's yard. My garden is on the other side of the house on that barren piece of sun-blistered, hardpan soil where the only tall green things growing are the weeds.

For years, I have started out each spring with dreams of the bountiful crops of juicy tomatoes, succulent corn, crisp carrots and green leafy lettuce I would produce. I'd look at the pictures on the seed packs down at my local nursery and I'd say to myself, "I can do that. I can grow things. I can feed my family delicious bowls of butter beans, peas and cherry tomatoes right from my own little piece of God's green earth."

I'd say this every year, despite the fact that in two decades of burying thousands of pounds of seeds, potato eyes, broccoli stems and other defenseless root plants in the ground, I've only produced a garden once that would make Martha Stewart proud of me.

# THINGS GROW, THEY DIE

Over the years, I've tried everything. I used to enrich the soil with nutrients, put on lime to sweeten it and mix in sand to make the land soft and loamy so the roots could breathe. Then, I'd follow the recommended planting schedules, all the while diligently watering, weeding and pruning until my hands were calloused and my back ached.

For about six weeks, everything would go well. The neat rows of carrot tops would come out of the ground and spring to attention, their little fluffy stems blowing in the breeze. The packets of hard-shelled dry beans would unfurl their helmet-shaped heads into beautiful green, leafy stocks. Alongside them, the tomato plants would reach for the sun, strong and healthy, lifting up their bright yellow flowers for all to see.

Just when I started to think, "This is it. This is the year I succeed," everything would fall over and die. That's not exactly true. Some years, the plants just withered and died without falling over. Other times, my garden would just get stripped bare by a plague of locusts.

It was always something. But every year, I pushed on, studying gardening and fertilizing books, seed catalogs and the latest books like, "Gardening for Dummies," but nothing ever worked. I've gone so far as to try old-fashioned techniques as well as some outlandish things. Once, I decided to try planting corn the Indian way by digging a hole, putting in a dead fish, then planting the corn seed on top. The corn grew up straight and tall with large ears of beautiful yellow corn, but no one would eat them. They smelled like fish and the fins growing out between the kernels were very unappetizing.

The next year, I said to myself, "The Amish seem to know what they're doing. I'll model myself after them." So, I grew a scraggly beard and put on a straw hat and began planting with a plow behind a team of horses. Nothing grew. On the plus side, though, I did get betrothed to the beautiful Katrina Van Patten, daughter of a wealthy Amish farmer. Her father promised me

500 acres and his daughter's hand in marriage. But, then he saw my garden and withdrew the offer, taking the horses and plow with him.

## THE DRUID WAY

The most unorthodox thing I ever tried was taking up the ancient Druid custom of planting seeds under a full moon, naked. I never found out if it worked. The police showed up while I was outside, and instead of trying to explain what I was doing dancing naked in the moonlight on top of a pile of manure with a pitchfork, I just said, "Arrest me, please. I'm insane."

The only time I ever produced a successful garden, it just happened. I was too busy to pull up the old plants that had withered in the garden the year before, and just left them there. The next spring—even though I hadn't planted anything—the garden sprouted and blossomed.

It was truly a wondrous garden with everything just growing wherever it felt like. I had peas in with the corn, and beans with the okra. Cucumbers and tomato plants and lettuce all grew side-by-side in some wonderful garden salad arrangement. I was in heaven when six weeks went by and nothing died.

I'll never forget the first harvest of green beans I brought in from my garden. The beans were so fresh and tasty, my family actually applauded my success. It was my finest gardening hour, and I felt a deep sense of pride and accomplishment as I watched my family devour the fruits of my labor.

The next night, I brought another bounty of luscious garden beans to the table, hot and brimming over the top of the bowl. Everybody looked from the beans to me in wonder and in one voice cried, "Do we have to eat beans again?"

That was the day I swore off gardening. Now, I just pass off my neighbor's garden as my own, and buy my produce at the local farmers market. It's simpler that way, and much less work.

*Don't people who become lawn and garden fanatics ever
wonder how all the flowers, grass and trees stayed
alive before there were plant doctors and
lawn-care specialists, and only God
to take care of them?*

## SURVIVING LAWN EXPERTS

I was doing some exercise the other day — clicking through the television channels with my remote control — when I came across a Public Broadcasting System program on garden and lawn care.

The show's host, Jerry Baker, was actually urging people to "shampoo" their lawn a couple times a summer. I don't know about you, but I think anybody who worries about their lawn needing a bath has too much time on their hands. In fact, I'm giving an open invitation to anyone who shampoos their lawn to come over to my house to cut my grass. They don't even have to wash it first.

The reason Baker encourages lawn shampooing is because he says it aids photosynthesis which helps the grass to grow. I have to say, I'm not very conversant about photosynthesis, but I'm pretty sure a little dirt on my grass is not going to keep it from growing.

Baker, I later found out, has a national following of people who want to learn the secrets of plant nurturing, including how to make grass grow faster. I'm the opposite. I spend a great deal of my time trying to encourage my lawn not to grow and I can't stop it. I mean I don't weed it. I don't fertilize it. I don't water it regularly. I don't do anything but cut the grass once-in-a-while and it still comes back every year.

Baker, on the other had, spends hours every week cutting his grass in a crisscross pattern so the grass roots don't get tanned by the sun. I can safely say my grass roots never see the sun because my method of lawn nurturing is to let the grass grow to about eight inches tall — to the point we start losing small puppies in it — and then I cut it.

## CAUGHT FEEDING THE LAWN

I myself gave up on gardening gurus with the homespun advice since I heard one on the radio say that the best way to get rid of moles in your yard is to put bubble gum in the tunnels because moles eat the stuff and explode or something. I tried using this technique but stopped when I overheard my one son confiding to his brother, "I think Dad's flipped out. I saw him out last night feeding bubble gum to the lawn."

Baker, who bills himself as "America's Master Gardener," is famous for his gardening recipes that use strange concoctions, including booze, birth control pills and tobacco products to cure plant and garden problems. One of his favorite all-purpose recipes for pest prevention calls for a mix of ammonia, dish detergent, castor oil and urine. It's supposed to keep your yard free of grubs, moles, deer, giant sloths and most of your neighbors.

Another recipe for lawn fertilizer includes a cup of bourbon. That's not too unusual, I've got a neighbor who has been using bourbon around his yard for years, except he doesn't spread it on the lawn. He drinks it. You can often hear him after a hard day of yard work talking to his grass, going "You're the most beautiful lawn in the world. I love you. Will you marry me?"

I found out, after reading up on Baker, that agriculture and gardening experts have labeled him a "pain in the petunia" because of his unorthodox  methods. In fact, one article I read said his ideas are being attacked by "angry horticulturists." Now there's a chilling thought. To me the term "angry horticulturists" conjures up images of Aunt Bea of Mayberry going after Baker with a garden hose because her roses died after she put some urine on them like he told her to do.

"Oh, Andy," cried Aunt Bea. "I think they withered away from shame over what I had done to them."

## GARDENING HAS BECOME CULT

I think people carry this gardening stuff to the extreme. It has become an obsession with some people. I saw where a guy in New Jersey was arrested seven times this summer for watering his yard during a drought that had the city fathers rationing water for drinking and bathing.

The guy, evidently, couldn't figure out how the police kept catching him, even though he had the only green lawn in the city. Another women went to the extreme of siphoning off water condensation from her neighbor's air conditioner and giving it to her shrubs to keep them alive. The neighbor took her to court over the incident. Surprisingly, the courts found this was not against any law.

Don't people who become lawn and garden fanatics ever wonder how all the flowers, grass and trees stayed alive before there were plant doctors and lawn-care specialists and only God took care of them?

When you stop to think about it, millions of people every year take vacations and spend billions of dollars to travel to national parks to see the beauty of this earth in its natural state. That must tell you something. I don't know of anyone who backpacks to the suburbs to look at manicured lawns.

*I found out one day that my squirrels were not only socking away food for winter, they had started shipping excess seed by UPS to cousins in Romania.*

## SURVIVING SQUIRRELS

I never used to think much about squirrels. They were always just there in the periphery of nature. Then one day I put up a bird feeder — or should I call it a squirrel diner — and the world changed.

In putting up the bird feeder, I had images of flocks of sparrows, titmice and turtle doves living in harmony in my back yard, happily chirping and cooing around my feeding station. Instead, what I got was a bunch of hairy thieves who are ruining my life.

I may be naive, but I thought everything in nature had a purpose. The birds spread seeds that propagate the forests. The bees pollinate the flowers. Even the butterflies color up our world. As near as I can figure out, all squirrels ever do is eat. And sometimes damage the battery cables of your car when you're trying to get to work in the dead of winter and it's 10 degrees outside.

These woodland thugs not only decimate the daily ration of bird seed I dollop out for our fine feathered friends, they have taken to terrorizing the neighborhood chickadees, often mugging them for the few kernels of millet in their beaks.

It is not a pretty sight when these treetop terrorists swoop down on my freshly filled feeder, scattering birds everywhere. Even the pugnacious blue jays take to the sky when they attack.

I realize most people like squirrels. They see those pudgy little cheeks, tiny paws, and fluffy tails and think squirrels are so cute. But it's all protective camouflage as far as I'm concerned.

I'm here to tell you that squirrel cheeks are pudgy because they're full of my bird seed, and probably some of yours, too. As for those cute little paws, well, they can rip out an eye if you get too close to them. And don't be fooled by those little fluffy tails squirrels have. They can wrap them around your arm and break your wrist in an instant if you ever grab a squirrel and try to strangle it.

## BACKYARD BATTLEFIELD

I have to tell you, my battle with squirrels has been going on since spring and I'm losing. At first, I tried pacification. I wrongly assumed there was enough bird feed in the world for all to share. But, after going through several 50-pound bags of seed in two weeks, the birds were dropping out of the trees from malnutrition, while the squirrels were growing fat. The early bird may get the worm, but the black oil sunflower seed belongs to the 7 a.m. squirrel.

I found out one day that my squirrels were not only socking away food for winter, they had started shipping excess seed by UPS to cousins in Romania.

To thwart these sneaky weasels, I took to hanging the bird feeders from lengthy ropes tossed over tree boughs. The squirrels laughed at me and merely slithered down the rope hand-over-hand to the feeders.

A friend suggested I install the feeders in an open area on metal pipes to which the wily squirrel could not get purchase to climb. This held them at bay for merely a day until they figured out how to tightrope walk across an overhead wire and leap to the top of the bird feeder.

I then strung a plastic wire across the yard, hanging the bird feeder in the middle and greasing the wire. I figured no squirrel would be able to get to my feeders now.

Wrong. The squirrels merely put on nonslip gloves and went crawling paw-over-paw across the wire. I thought briefly of electrifying the wire as a squirrel preventative, but images of fried nut hatches dissuaded me.

Not being able to outwit these tree-climbing rodents, I checked out squirrel preventatives in a nature book. It suggested I add cayenne pepper to the bird seed. This burning spice has no effect on birds, but gives a hotfoot of the mouth to squirrels.

I watched in glee as first one squirrel then the next munched on my hot tamale mix, only to dive from the feeder and go chattering into the woods. I thought I had won the battle, only to discover the next day that they had taken to scattering seeds on the ground and waiting for the rain to wash off the hot sauce.

## GOING SQUIRRELLY

By now, several months had gone by and my feasting fur balls had grown to the size of well-fed house cats. They had gotten so big, they could no longer scamper and forage fecklessly through the trees. Instead, they took to hanging around the bird feeder, smoking cigarettes and throwing dice for their daily ration of nuts and berries.

What was worse, the squirrels no longer had a fear of me or my cunning collie. In fact, one night I found my poor dog bound and gagged, whimpering underneath the bird feeder, a threatening note attached to her collar, warning me to keep her chained — or else.

I should have taken that as a warning that things had escalated. The next night when I went out with my bird seed, three squirrels mugged me and stole the bag of seed right out of my hands.

After that incident, I thought I would just stop putting out bird seed for a while, to encourage the sneak thieves to move on to seedier pastures. All it did was infuriate the squirrels. They took to gnawing on my Buick Electra, damaging a quarter panel and several fenders. One day, I came out to find my tires gnawed through with the telltale odor of nut breath lingering around the vehicle.

As a last resort before we became prisoners in our own house, I decided to get rid of this squirrelly bunch once and for all. I brought in a professional squirrel catcher who would humanely trap the varmints and release them in someone else's yard. To my dismay, the only thing the traps managed to capture was my collie, who looked pretty embarrassed when we found her.

Unfortunately, the one surefire squirrel solution I know would work, small arms weaponry is not permitted in our neighborhood. So for now, we live with an uneasy truce with our rodent friends, while I ply them with generous portions of fatty peanuts in hopes that they'll someday drop dead from all of the cholesterol.

*From personal experience, I have found*
*the hardest part of deck construction*
*is getting other people to help*
*you with the project.*

# SURVIVING DECK BUILDING

The summer season is upon us. And around our house, that means it's time to get out the hammer, saws and nails and other sharp, pointy objects that can puncture the skin and cut off limbs for my semiannual attempt at deck building.

It's hard to believe that ten years ago I knew absolutely nothing about building decks. I can still remember the fateful day my wife, Madeline, suggested it would be a wonderful idea for us to build a deck off our bedroom so we could enjoy breakfasts on the deck on Sunday mornings and a glass of iced tea there on hot summer nights.

She showed me a picture of the deck she had in mind. It was a photograph cut from one of those "beautiful homes" magazines, in which rich people hire skilled carpenters to create architectural wonders in their back yards. The deck my wife wanted me to build was a three-level sun deck, with curving staircase, built-in benches, flower boxes and a gazebo.

I suggested we find another house that already had a deck like that, get new jobs so we could afford to buy it and move all of our things there. I figure that would be easier than trying to build a deck that looked like it might be a challenge to Frank Lloyd Wright.

I have to admit, trying to build a deck — which had to look good and yet be structurally sound enough to hold people and patio furniture without falling apart — scared me.

My history with building things was limited to a tree fort I once built as a kid and a garden shed that came in a kit that my children helped me build.

## DON'T TRY THIS AT HOME

When I was about 10, my friends and I built this tree fort out of old, unused railway ties we had found abandoned beside the train tracks in the railroad yard near our homes. It took us three weeks to haul about six tons of railway ties up into this small oak tree and build a fort any kid would love.

The fort had turrets and lookout towers and a draw bridge, and we were the envy of all our friends for exactly one day, until the tree collapsed under the weight of the fort. Stupid tree.

The garden shed turned out lots better. It came in a kit of pre-cut wood, with a roof, floor, doors and all the hardware needed to build it. On the cover of the instruction manual was a picture of a father, standing with his 6- and 10-year-old sons, proudly looking at the shed.

So, I gathered my six-and ten-year-old sons next to me with the shed material, handed them the manual and said "go to it, boys" and they built us a shed just like the one in the picture.

By the time my first deck building project rolled around, the boys had become much older and wiser and disappeared from the house for a week.

Actually, the first deck turned out pretty well. It was to be a nice 8-by-10-foot deck off a patio door from our bedroom. It turned out a 10-by-35-foot deck that wrapped around half of the lower level of the house.

"Why did you have to make it so big?" asked my wife after the deck was completed.

"It was a mistake by the lumber yard," I explained. "They incorrectly sent me the exact amount of wood I ordered."

"Oh," she said, accepting my explanation with a confused look on her face. Then she asked, "Is it supposed to lean like that on purpose?"

"We can plant bushes around it and no one will notice," I suggested.

## "I'LL BUILD THAT DECK"

You'd think after that experience, I'd never have to level another 2 by 4 board or figure out how to get a square post in a round hole again. But you'd be wrong. From that first attempt, deck building got into my blood.

When we were building our first home, I righteously crossed off the measly 100-square-foot deck the builder was going to put on our new home and announced, "I'll build the deck myself."

Two years later, after studying hundreds of deck plans from a vast variety of deck construction magazines and taking numerous pictures of decks friends had built that didn't collapse, I was ready to launch my project.

It was going to be a two-level deck, with 900 square feet of floor space, rail guards, flower boxes and built-in benches. When I was done, people would come from miles around to marvel at what I had accomplished.

I'll never forget how I felt the morning the lumber company delivered the materials. I looked at the 10-foot-high pile of timbers, steps, hand rail parts and flooring, and thought to myself, "My God, what have I gotten myself into?"

From personal experience, I have found the hardest part of deck construction is getting other people to help you with the project. Once again, my sons disappeared when I announced I was going to build a deck — one decided on the spur of the moment to go for his master's degree and the other joined the Army.

Friends and neighbors, though, were much more willing to pitch in and lend a hand. I found all I had to do to get help was sink a couple 18-foot deck posts in the ground crooked — some leaning out at a 45 degree angle— and then call over my neighbor and go, "John, do those look straight to you?"

All kinds of people rushed to my aid.

And everyone brought with them their own skill. Some people were good at measuring boards. A few could use the circular saw without cutting off fingers. Others even had the skill to hammer nails straight. In no time at all — roughly six months and 14 days — my hearty crew and I had finished the deck project.

As we stood beside one another admiring our handiwork in building the dual-level, 900-square-foot deck with hand rails, and future spots where built-in flower boxes and benches would go, my wife, Madeline, came out and was exuberant with praise.

"It's beautiful," she said. "But is it supposed to lean like that on purpose?"

*Growing up, I never had any experience with hunting or hunters. I was raised in a city where guns were primarily used for their constitutional purpose — to take out street lights and for drive-by shootings.*

## SURVIVING DEER STALKING

This weekend, an estimated 600,000 usually normal people will leave the shelter of their warm and cozy homes to go out into the woods and blast a bunch of deer into freezer meat.

Don't get me wrong, I don't have anything against deer hunters. My personal philosophy is I never say anything bad about people who wear hats with ear flaps and sit in the dark with loaded guns. For one thing, I have no background to be judgmental about such things. I've only gone hunting once, and I slept through most of it.

Growing up, I never had any experience with hunting or hunters. I was raised in a city where guns were primarily used for their constitutional purpose —to take out street lights and for drive-by shootings. The closest I ever came to hunting wild animals was once going out with a bunch of my 11-year-old friends to shoot at squirrels in a city park. Luckily, we got stopped by the police who confiscated the World War II rifles, German Luger handguns and grenades we were carrying, before we hurt ourselves or some unsuspecting streetlights.

So, I knew virtually nothing about hunting until I was 35 when my friend, Lester, asked me to go hunting with him and some of his buddies.  I accepted the invitation with reluctance. Not knowing anything about hunting, I didn't want to make a fool of myself in front of these seasoned hunters and do something stupid, like show up at camp in  an orange vest and hat with ear flaps, so I decided to do some research on the subject first. What I found out is that  750,000 people in Michigan go deer hunting annually.

The majority of these hunters, 600,000 or more, use rifles, shotguns and heavy artillery for this sport. About 100,000 use the more challenging bows and arrows, and another 50,000 hunt with flintlock rifles that have to be manually loaded with black powder just like Daniel Boone did when he went hunting here in Michigan. There are also a few naturalist out there who like to hunt with Bowie knives and take their annual deer by dropping out of a tree on it and fighting the bewildered animal in hand-to-hoof combat.

## THE COST OF THE HUNT

I further discovered that deer hunters — in addition to knocking off at least a couple deer a season — spend $500 million each year to do it, or the equivalent of $5 million per deer. The breakdown of hunting purchases each year is $50 million for guns and ammunition, $40 million for food, clothing and lures, and $10 million for licenses. They spend the other $400 million on beer.

Oh, I almost forgot, hunters also spend a whopping $30 to $40 a season on accommodations, as evidenced by the place we stayed during my one hunting trip. Somehow, I got the impression that we were going to be staying at a "rustic hunting cabin" up north. I pictured this cozy little cottage tucked away in the woods, with a stone fireplace, some deer antlers on the wall for decoration, maybe hand-hewn wilderness furniture to relax on and, of course, running water, electricity, a color TV and maybe indoor plumbing.

We wound up staying in a lean-to somebody had built out of wooden packing crates. It was a 150-square-foot box with five bunk beds, and a cast iron stove for cooking and heat. The only running water in the place was a leak in the roof.

The rustic furniture in the cabin was a big square table made out of two plywood doors nailed to tree stumps. And as for decorations on the wall, the only things hanging there were flattened beer cans nailed in place for insulation.

"I saw a 'Motel 6' up the highway about 50 miles," I suggested as we entered our weekend retreat. "I could check it out and be back in the morning."

"No time for that," I was assured. "We've got to get ready for Opening Day." The procedure for getting ready for Opening Day consisted of "opening" some hot dogs, beans and beer, and playing cards until 2 a.m.

## REAL MEN DON'T HUNT

Now, up to this point in time, I always thought when men went hunting, they went hunting. I didn't exactly know what they did, but I expected it was something along the line of stalking tigers with people banging garbage can lids together to flush the antelope out of the woods. That's the way we did it where I grew up. I didn't realize deer hunting primarily consisted of sitting in the dark, freezing, with a gun in your hands. I didn't need to go into the woods to do that, I could have just stayed at the cabin and accomplished the same thing.

The only memorable moment that stands out in my mind about my first day of hunting was being offered a splash of (you're not going to believe this) doe urine as cologne.

"You guys are sick," I told my friend, but he assured me it was an old hunting trick.

"The scent attracts bucks who are interested in mating to your position," my friend explained.

He found it hard to believe, but I declined the offer.

"None for me, thanks," I said. "I don't want any amorous buck sneaking up behind me when I'm not looking."

Instead, my friend Lester gave me some old deer antlers I could click together to make the sound of deer combat, which he promised would bring a big buck into sight attracted to the animal's other main interest — fighting. That's just what I wanted, a lure to attract a large-horned, wild animal out of the woods looking to fight with me.

Finally, I just set up shop in a thicket overlooking a deer trail with no doe scent or clicking antlers, just me and the great outdoors. I sat there watching this empty patch of ground for five hours. The only deer I saw that day was when I fell asleep and dreamed this big 12 point buck came out of the woods and asked me for a date.

# Chapter 4
# SURVIVING YOUR LIFE

*Turning 50 can be traumatic. Your memory starts to go but on the positive side, you're always meeting new people. At 50 you start looking forward to "early bird" dinners and family outings at Sam's Club. House cleaning is easier as your eyesight goes because you can't see the dust even if the garden trolls haven't hidden your glasses.*

*It's kind of crazy, but since hitting 50, I've really gotten into "Golden Girls" reruns, which I never used to watch. That Bea Arthur is such a fox.*

# SURVIVING TURNING 50

I had a birthday this week. It was the big 5 - 0!

Actually, I don't really think I should classify as a 50-year-old, because as a youngster I was sickly for about three years and didn't get out much, so I don't think I should count those years against my age. And I don't remember much about what went on between the time I was born until about 1954, so I wouldn't hold that time against me either.

The same would apply to 1983 to 1987, when my short-term memory went on vacation. I have no recollection of that time, except from photographs.

I also think I should be able to subtract all of the bad days I've had at work over the years. I certainly wouldn't call time wasted at budget meetings, team building seminars and strategic planning sessions as quality time. And if I take out all of the years I spent in elementary school, high school and college, learning things I've since forgotten, I figure I'm about 17 right now and ready to party, just as long as I don't stay out late, avoid fatty foods and don't overdo it on too many sodas.

## PROS/CONS OF TURNING 50

But there are pros and cons to turning 50. I think the worst part of turning 50 is all those birthday cards you get with "50" written on them. For some reason, these cards usually have "50" spelled out on them in 8-inch-tall letters, in case you can't see them or you've forgotten that 50 years have passed since the last time someone held you upside down naked, and slapped you on the butt. Well, it's been 50 years since that happened to me. I don't know about the rest of you out there.

Another thing I don't like about turning 50 is finally having to admit I've reached middle age, more or less. For some reason, the anticipation of turning 50 and getting my AARP card just doesn't have the same excitement I had at 16, looking forward to receiving my driver's license. I also don't like the fact that my eyebrows are growing up my forehead to occupy the place where my hairline used to be.

It's also disheartening when young women call me "sir" and offer to help me cross the street. That really hurts. I'm also not too excited about getting my "Senior Citizen" discount card in the mail. However, getting into the movies for half-price on "seniors" night could have its advantages.

The good thing about reaching 50 is I don't have to worry about ever doing it again. I guess the fact that I'm still kicking is a plus. It's better than the alternative.

On the positive side, I can now try out for the Professional Golf Association "Seniors" Golf Tour, if my back gets better and my arthritis doesn't act up — and I learn to play golf.

I can also forget things with impunity these days, and people will blame it on my age. And, now that I'm older, my peculiar personal idiosyncrasies have become "amusing character traits" and "eccentric foibles" instead of just being "annoying habits." Plus, once you're past 50, people approach you for the wisdom you can give them. Don't they?

## 'EARLY BIRD' DINNER ANYONE?

Some things in life do change at 50, and I believe it's a natural part of the aging process. For example, since turning 50 I've had this sudden urge to go out and catch "Early Bird" dinner specials from 4 to 5:30 p.m. daily. I've also developed a fondness for Bermuda shorts and white knee socks. Also, I talk to my dog more these days — "Don't I, little poochie woochie?"

One of the things I hate about being 50 is that time keeps ticking on and I still have lots of things to do. I also wish I'd taken better care of myself when I was younger, advice I've passed on to my kids, but I don't think they're listening.

The bad thing about hitting 50 is not being able to ever see the loved ones again who passed on before me. I also miss the good friends I lost touch with over the years. Maybe I should give them a call. I also miss throwing a 93 mph fast ball, not that I ever could, but I'm sure somebody who turned 50 must have done that sometime.

It's kind of crazy, but since hitting 50, I've really gotten into "Golden Girls" reruns, which I never used to watch. That Bea Arthur is such a fox.

On the other hand, I now feel like I'm a peeping Tom when I turn into "Bay Watch" to see what kind of trouble "Mitch" and the gang have gotten themselves into this week. Just recently, Mitch and the other life guards had to deal with budget reductions at the station. He helped save everybody's job by cutting back on material on the bathing suits the girls wear.

It's also tough on me adjusting to the thought that my little boys are now men, adults with their own lives beyond our home. Since turning 50, things my parents used to say keep creeping into my conversations with my kids, like "turn down that noise, and turn up the heat on my warm milk."

Worse, I've had to stop myself several times from using that phrase passed down from one generation to the next since the beginning of time. The phrase I keep promising myself I won't ever say to my kids, but I know someday I will utter those immortal words ... "when I was your age ..."

If I ever say that guys, don't listen. It's just my age talking. Heck, I wish I were still your age. But I can't be, so have fun, kids, 50 is just around the corner.

*Once, my missing wallet turned up in a pillow case in the clothes washer. I have a sneaking suspicion someone in this house was trying to launder money.*

## SURVIVING WANDERING THINGS

Could you help me find my glasses? They were on my nose a minute ago and now they've totally disappeared.

And that's about the third time they've done that in the past hour. I think there's something wrong with them. They never used to act this way. They used to be very well-behaved glasses that stayed where they were placed, whether on the bridge of my nose, the top of my head or in a shirt pocket.

Now, they seem to have developed this desire to roam around the house.

Yesterday, they just up and left for three hours for no reason. I tore the house apart looking for them, which is not easy since I couldn't see anything. I finally found my glasses in the ice tray in the freezer. Why they wanted to hide out in the freezer is beyond me.

It was just plain dumb luck that I found them there at all. I just happened to be looking in the freezer for my wallet and there were my glasses sitting on top of an Eskimo Pie box. I haven't a clue how they opened the freezer door, climbed in and shut it. But they did. I really have no other explanation.

While my glasses like to wander around the house, my wallet is a different story. It likes to dematerialize from my pants pocket and show up in odd places in the house. Just the other day it disappeared from my pocket and then rematerialized on a soap dish in the shower.

My wallet tends to stay close to home. When it disappears, it turns up hiding in old suits or sometimes the silverware drawer. Once, my wallet turned up in a pillow case in the clothes washer. I have a sneaking suspicion someone in this house was trying to launder money.

# CHECKBOOK FORAGING

The problem with my glasses disappearing started about two years ago. I think it was two years ago, maybe it was more. But I know it was right around the time someone started hiding my car keys.

Like I said, my glasses were well-behaved up until that point. I'd be reading a book, set them down on the end table and they'd stay there.

Then for no reason, they began wandering off to parts unknown, just like my checkbook did.

Now, disappearing glasses are one thing, but wandering checkbooks are something else entirely. I mean, I can always buy another pair of glasses, but without a checkbook, how am I going to pay for them?

The most unnerving thing about my checkbook disappearing from time-to-time is that whoever takes it, forges my name on checks and pays my bills with it. I'll tell you, it gets downright spooky to know someone else can have access to my checkbook at any time and they can do a perfect forgery of my signature. The worst part is, whoever is doing this always forgets to enter the checks into the register.

The last time this happened, I was going to call up my bank and tell them to open a new account for me. I would have done it too, but I couldn't remember what bank it was. And then whoever took my checkbook, returned it. They hid it in one of my golf shoes in the trunk of my car.

I know what you're thinking. You're thinking that what's happening with my glasses and wallet and checkbook is that I'm probably getting a little forgetful as I get older, but that's not the case and I can prove it. I couldn't have left the checkbook in the trunk of my car because my car keys were stolen last week and I didn't have any keys to open the trunk. So, whoever took my car keys is probably the same person who stole the checkbook and hid it in my golf shoes in the trunk.

# TROLLS ARE SUSPECTED

Actually, I'm not the only one having this problem in our house. My wife, Madeline, also goes through periods where things just disappear.

She solved the wandering eyeglass problem, though, by buying multiple sets of those reading glasses you can purchase at finer convenience stores around the area. Then she just sort of "salts" a couple dozen or so around the house, so no matter what room they roam to, she has a good chance of finding a pair hiding somewhere near the place she thought she left them.

I think the problem we have at our place is that we have gotten an infestation of "garden trolls" in the house.

You know what garden trolls are, don't you? They are those pesky little critters that hide out around your house playing mischievous tricks on you. Like, you go to work in the morning and find a garden troll has left your car door open, killing the battery. Their favorite trick is to roll your car window down on the driver's side on nights that it rains.

I know they do this because they've done it to me on any number of occasions.

But garden trolls, if kept outside, are really very little problem. Oh, they might move a rake out of the tool shed once in a while and lay it in the driveway where a car might run over it, puncturing two tires and causing $200 in repairs, but on the whole they seem content to tie knots in the garden hose, leave your car door and windows open and tip over bird baths.

But once a garden troll gets in your house, look out. They like to take things and hide them. Glasses, wallets, checkbooks, dinner dishes, clothes, they just run rampant once they get in.

I just found an article in this month's Reader's Digest on "How to Get Garden Trolls Out of Your House." The secret is.....

Hey, who took my magazine?

*We did have one girl at the reunion who honestly had not changed a bit since college. Doreen is still a size five and hasn't aged a year. We decided she must have made a pact with the devil.*

# SURVIVING THE CLASS REUNION

It's spring. The season for class reunions.

I went to a reunion last weekend, and I've got to say it was much better than most of the ones I have attended before. In the past, I'd go to a reunion and I wouldn't know anyone. This time, though, I went to a reunion of people I actually went to school with, so I knew more people.

This was a 30th reunion of my college journalism and media buddies. It had been three decades since we had last been together, and I really wanted to be there because some of them still owed me money.

One of things we did at this reunion that I thought was neat was we put everyone's name in 1-inch-tall letters on our name tags so we didn't have to spend three days squinting at each other's chest. The other memory aid we used was putting our old photos on the name tags.

Since I couldn't find any old pictures of me, I used the next best thing. I stuck a picture of Leonardo DiCaprio on my name tag. People would walk up to me look at my picture and burst out laughing for some reason.

One of the young waitresses who was serving at our re-union dinner looked at my picture and said, "Did you know you looked just like Leonardo DiCaprio when you were younger?"

I said, "Yes, and I wish I still looked like that now." With a straight face, she replied. "You do. You've just gotten a lot more rounder."

Actually, I got the idea for my name tag when I looked at the name tags of some friends, Barb and Kevin, who had gotten married after college. They had a picture of themselves when they were a young couple. I have to say, I honestly didn't realize how much they looked like Tom Cruise and Nicole Kidman when they were younger until I saw their name tag pictures.

## WOMEN GETTING BLONDER

I also noticed a strange phenomena at this reunion. As we've gotten older, the men's hair has gotten grayer while the women we went to school with have almost all turned to blondes. It must have something to do with hormones.

It's funny how things you did when you were younger stick with you. One guy, Wally, managed a pizza place when were in college. Everyone at the reunion asked him if he was still in the pizza business. He was kind of put off. "Is that all anybody remembers of me. Pizzas? I've done other things in my life." Like what, Wally? "I owned a restaurant for 20 years. Now I'm in food distribution."

Richard, the photographer, still had the ever-present camera in front of his face. What we all remember of him was that he was always taking pictures. When he took the camera down from his face at the reunion, no one recognized him.

There were other changes in the group. Linda the "go-go" queen of the dance floor, who used to boogie to every song all night long, had to sit out every third record for pulmonary resuscitation. Also, a lot of the guys like George, who used to wear their hair long and curly, have opted for shorter hair these days, usually cut way back to a few strands on top in a style that men in their 40s and 50s seem to favor.

We did have one girl at the reunion who honestly had not changed a bit since college. Doreen still wears a size five and hasn't aged a year. We decided she must have made a pact with the devil.

As a group, we discovered we could still party until 3 a.m. Especially if we got up late the next day and took a two-hour nap in the afternoon.

## TALKING DRUG USE

One of the things that was different from 30 years ago was that now we could openly talk about our drug use. Not that we did anything illegal back then. Maybe a cola and an aspirin now and again. This time around, the only "highs" we talked about usually had "blood pressure" or "cholesterol" put in front of them

There was a big discussion one night about a hot new drug mixture that is going around for older people. It blends Viagra, which is sort of a catnip for men, with the natural memory aid Ginkoba. Since I have no short-term memory and don't use Ginkoba, I forget what this drug is supposed to do for you.

Two of our group had become doctors. One is a physician and the other a sex therapist. Coincidentally, they are both named 'Judy' which caused a little confusion at one point in the reunion.

On the second day of the festivities, one of our people got food poisoning symptoms after breakfast and took violently ill. Thinking quickly, we offered to call "Dr. Judy," the physician, to help diagnose the problem. The patient, though, thought we meant the other Dr. Judy. Doubled up in pain, she cried out, "Look, I'm sick: I'm not sexually dysfunctional."

The last night of the reunion was probably the best. There were about 80 of us at a dinner and dance, including some of our former college faculty, who were claiming we still owed them term papers.

As we sat around our table, I looked down the line and everyone there looked like we did 30 years ago. Only this time, it was as if we all got together as youngsters and decided to get made up to see what we would look like if we were older.

The nice thing about getting back together with old friends is that it's as if we just left off talking yesterday, even if yesterday was 30 years ago. In the end, I realized none of us had really changed. We're all still 20-year-olds in our hearts.

*Friends, who were Sam's Club members, would make us feel*
*as if we were failing the free enterprise system*
*by not being on Sam's team.*

## SURVIVING SAM'S CLUB

I didn't want to do it, but after years of suffering verbal public ridicule for my unpopular stand, I finally went out and did it. I got my "Sam's Club" membership.

For those of you who are not familiar with Sam's Club, it is one of those deep discount megastores where you go in planning to buy a few light bulbs and maybe some lunch snacks and come out two hours later with several bulging shopping carts and a cash register receipt for $278.29.

And that's the reason I've avoided the place all these years. You see I'm a bargain junkie. I can't pass up a bargain, no matter how useless and unneeded the product. If it's on sale, it's in my cart. I once bought a gerbil cage at a yard sale because it was marked "50 percent off." Which was really not very smart, since not only did I not need a gerbil cage, but everything at a yard sale is at least "50 percent off."

So, I've been avoiding being a Sam's Club member for at least a dozen years. And it has been embarrassing. I'd go to family picnics or holiday dinners, and that's all people were talking about — shopping at Sam's Club.

"See this turkey we're having for Thanksgiving," my Aunt Stella, the bargain hunter, would say. "I got it for 29 cents a pound at Sam's Club.

"See this turkey baster, it was $1.29 at Sam's Club. These giblets, they came free with the 29-cents-a-pound turkey from Sam's Club," Aunt Stella would announce.

"That's nothing," boasted my cousin, DeeDee. "We stopped at Sam's Club on the way over and outfitted the entire family for a three-week camping trip at Yellowstone National Park at Sam's Club for just $589.29."

## THE SAM'S CLUB WAY

Other relatives had furnished their entire homes for $14,331.29 with a one-stop shopping trip to Sam's Club.

"And, we saved enough money to start a college fund for our son," said cousin, Mike, proudly.

Eventually, someone would get around to my wife and I, and innocently ask, "And what have you two bought lately at Sam's Club?"

My wife, Madeline, and I would look at each other uneasily and try to change the subject with some diversionary comment like, "Did you all know our son, Nathan, got married this past summer?"

And everyone would sit there, waiting expectantly for us to finish our story. Finally, cousin John or someone would prompt us with, "And so how much did you save at Sam's Club on the wedding?" Eventually, it would come out that we, in fact, were not Sam's Club members, and when they learned this, our family disowned us.

They weren't the only ones to do this. Friends, who were Sam's Club members, would make us feel as if we were failing the free enterprise system by not being on Sam's team.

"This is how communism starts," one told us. "Plus, you missed a great sale on pot roast last week."

But, we are now part of Sam's Club, with our own "Sam's Club Advantage Member" card with its motto, "The Secret to Living Well..." right next to my out-of-focus picture.

The local Sam's Club is a giant warehouse with huge shelving units displaying almost everything any human being would want to purchase in one shopping trip. I mean, you can do your weekly grocery shopping there, outfit a home office and get your car tires changed in a single trip, and all at discount prices.

## BUYING HAS PRIVILEGE

To get the privilege of shopping there, you have to buy a membership card for $35, which allows you to spend as much money as you like filling your house with Sam's Club stuff.

On our first trip through the store, Madeline and I discovered the Sam's Club secret to living well. You have to buy mass quantities of everything on your shopping list. The store doesn't sell anything in ones and twos. It's 16 toothbrushes or nothing. Which is the worst thing you can do to a bargain shopper.

"We don't need 16 toothbrushes," Madeline said as I put a five-year supply of toothbrushes into our cart.

"Yeah, but did you see the price per unit on these babies? They're only $1.29 each in bulk. We just saved at least $8.29 with this one purchase," I said, getting into the feel of the game.

"Yes, but it cost $21 to do it and we only needed one $2 toothbrush," she replied.

It went like this throughout the store as I heaped more bargains into first one shopping cart and then a second.

"Hey, look," I cried, going into the meat section. "Here's a 50 pound bag of pork chops for just $1.29 a pound. Do you think we should buy two packages?"

In addition to the pork chops and toothbrushes, I also bought 30 pounds of hot dogs, a gallon of mustard, 300 hot dog buns, a 17 pound bag of potato chips, a dozen yards of smoked sausage, a dinner service for 24 people, a complete 18 piece deck and patio set, a family room recliner, portable welder and a gerbil cage (Hey it was 50 percent off and my other gerbil cage is getting lonely, OK?).

And, it all came to only $2,444.29. I can't wait to go back next week and save even more money. Plus, the best part is now I will be allowed back into the family.

*Women will search out things to clean, while men do anything to avoid housework, including inventing stuff like the dishwasher, self-cleaning oven, the microwave and paper plates.*

# SURVIVING HOUSEWORK

Who does more housework, men or women? That question was recently asked of 1,000 men and women across the U.S.A.

A whopping 90 percent of the women said they did more housework than men. On the male side, 75 percent of men responded, "What's housework?"

Right now, every married woman out there is poking her husband in the ribs, saying, "See, I told you so," while the guys are giving each other the high fives, going, "Good answer."

Being both married, and a guy who just got poked in the ribs by his wife, I can say I sympathize with women. There is no doubt in my mind that women do more housework than men. The reason for this is that women have an ability to see dirt, often sense dirt, that is invisible to the human eye. They also have the urge to want to do something about it.

Guys, on the other hand, can only see dirt when it is pointed out to them, usually by a woman, and even then sometimes they are unable to see it.

As an example, the other day my wife, Madeline, without warning pointed at our kitchen windows and announced, "The windows are dirty. We need to wash them." I, as the man of the house, looked right through the glass at the blurry woodland creatures frolicking in the back yard — I think they were penguins — and said, "Why? I can still see daylight through them."

And that is the crux of the housework issue between men and women. Where women see things that need to be done, men haven't a clue anything needs cleaning until they go to wash the family dog and find out they've been feeding and walking a giant dust bunny for the past two years.

## DNA CLEANING GENE

The reason for this, as discovered in research conducted by the Windex Institute of North Dakota Extension, is that women have a cleaning chromosome attached to their DNA. This is attached in the exact same spot of the DNA chain where men have what looks like, under high-powered magnification, a beer tap. Scientists believe this is a clue as to why women want to clean and men want to lie on the sofa and watch football.

As an example, if a woman sees dirty dishes piled up in the sink, she will have a pathological urge to wash them — or at least hide them in the dishwasher. A man, on the other hand, carrying a dirty plate to the sink and finding it full, realizes there is still room on the counter for more dishes.

Men do this knowing full well that some person of another gender with a cleaning chromosome will come along and wash them. The other gender doesn't even have to be someone who lives in the house. I've seen my mother stop at a friend's house and do their dishes. Sometimes, she'll drop in on strangers and go, "Oh, I just popped in to wash your dishes. Hope you don't mind."

While a sink full of dirty dishes is a pretty obvious sign that something needs to be done there, like covering them with a dish towel, other home-cleaning needs are less noticeable to men.

My wife and I can look at the same piece of furniture in our living room and she'll see dust that needs to be wiped away, while I only see a bright, clean surface.

"Look at that dust," she'll say, and I'll be going, "What dust? Where?" Then, she'll move a lamp or something and expose a layer of dust that is totally invisible to the male eye.

I'll go, "Sure, when you move that lamp, you can see it, but otherwise it's not there, unless, of course, you write your initials in it like you're doing right now."

# WOMEN FIND DIRT

The problem is, women have this penchant for finding dirt in places no one ever sees, or goes. They'll move whole rooms of furniture to find dirt that men would never notice if someone didn't move the furniture and point it out to them.

That's the big difference between men and women. Women will search out things to clean, while men do anything to avoid housework, including inventing things like the dishwasher, self-cleaning oven, microwave and paper plates.

Women, on the other hand, love things that require extra work. They like fine crystal that needs to be hand-washed and furniture and knickknacks that collect dust.

This even applies to science. Today, men are busy scouting the solar system for planets you couldn't get to in 5 million years to clean, while women researchers are uncovering microscopic organisms that live in bed linens that can only be killed through lots of work.

The other day, I walked into our bedroom and Madeline had the entire bed torn apart and was vacuuming the mattress. So I asked the obvious question, "Why are you vacuuming the mattress?"

"I'm trying to kill the dust mites," she said. "They're everywhere and we may have to sanitize the whole house to get rid of them," she added, getting that look on her face which usually means heavy furniture moving is involved.

"I'd like to help but I've got to take the dog to the vet. I think something's wrong with her," I said, holding up a dust bunny on a dog leash. "I took her for a walk this morning and she kept blowing away in the wind."

*I plugged up the vacuum when I was cleaning out my car after
the birdseed bag broke while I was fixing a muffler clamp.
It was an afternoon I'd rather forget.*

# SURVIVING HOME REPAIR

My spouse is always wondering why repairs never get done around the house. I have to disagree with her. I get a lot of things accomplished, She just doesn't notice them.

To prove it to her, I kept track of all the things I did one recent Saturday while she was out.

The day started with her reminder that the light bulb over the kitchen sink needed to be replaced. So, after breakfast, I headed to the garage to get the step ladder needed to reach the bulb which hangs from a bare wire above the kitchen sink. I won't get into explaining why the bulb is hanging from a bare wire, because that's another story that really has nothing to do with why things never get done around our house.

Anyway, I'm out in the garage trying to get the step ladder free from the accumulation of "stuff" that has piled itself in front of the ladder when I come across the new furnace filter I was supposed to install last fall. Since it's almost the middle of February, I decide I better do that job first, and head for the basement storage room where we keep the furnace.

On the way there, I pass by the dehumidifier, which we use to take the moisture out of the air, and find it has shut off because the water bucket inside is full. So, I put the furnace filter down and take the water bucket over to the bathroom to empty it.

As I'm about to pour the water down the drain, I notice a section of wallpaper that came loose several years ago that I've been meaning to glue back in place. I realize I better get that done before I forget again. Setting the water pail down, I go back upstairs to the utility closet where we keep the glue. As I'm rummaging through the closet, I come across the silicone spray, which

I need to fix the squeak in the hinges of our bedroom door, sitting right next to the glue.

I take the glue out and set it on the floor in the hallway so it will be easier to find later when I go to tack up the wallpaper in the bathroom where I've left the dehumidifier water, which needs to be dumped before I replace the furnace filter that I found getting the step ladder to change the kitchen light bulb hanging on that bare wire.

In the bedroom, behind the squeaking door, I find a painting we received as a gift 25 years ago on our wedding day that I've been meaning to put up. It won't take more than five minutes to hang it, so I set the silicone spray on the bedroom nightstand and head to my workshop to get my tools. On the way back to our bedroom, I notice the bannister on the stairs is loose, which is dangerous, so I stop to do some momentary adjustments to the railing —since I have tools with me.

Just then, the phone rings, and I run up the stairs to answer it. It's my son's friend. He wants to leave a message for him. I go to get a pen and paper out of the cabinet drawer, which, as usual, is stuck. I pull the whole thing out and set it on the kitchen table, thinking while I've got the tools out to tighten the bannister and hang the picture, I might as well fix the drawer.

## MR. FIXIT STRIKES AGAIN

To get to the part of the drawer that needs fixing, which is on the bottom, I have to dump all the stuff out onto the kitchen table. Just as I suspected, the drawer needs to be clamped and glued. Since the bathroom with the falling wallpaper was on the way to my workshop, I figured I'd take the drawer with me, pick up the glue, stop off and fix the wallpaper, empty the dehumidifier water, then clamp the drawer.

Down in the bathroom, I had to stand on the toilet seat to reach the wallpaper that was coming down. As I stood on the lid of the toilet, the rusty bolts that I've been meaning to fix for a decade or so finally gave way and the toilet seat broke. "No problem," I figure, I've had the stuff to fix it in my screw-and- bolt cabinet since Reagan was in office.

I'll just go get the bolts, come back, fix the toilet, paste up the wallpaper, empty the dehumidifier water, glue the drawer, change the furnace filter, tighten the bannister, hang the picture, spray the squeak, get the ladder and change the bulb, and I'll be all done.

While rummaging around for the bolts for the toilet, guess what I find. It's the stereo adapter that I bought two years ago when we got our new television that will allow us to hear movies in stereo. That'll take only about a minute or two to hook up. So, I go to put the adapter on. The only problem is, we have one of those entertainment wall units, and you have to take everything out to connect anything.

Shrugging my shoulders, I take out the stereo receiver, the VCR, the tuner and the television set, all of which I neatly place on the floor in our living room. I get everything hooked up, but as I'm preparing to put stuff back I realize the wire to the speakers isn't going to be long enough to reach the stereo, so I've got to move the couch away from the wall to reposition the speakers so I can get everything tucked back into the cabinet.

## THERE'S THE BIRDSEED

We don't move the couch very much because it's big and heavy, and underneath I find a couple months worth of dust and debris. Thinking while I have the sofa out, and before I can finishing repairing the stereo and put it back together, I best go get the vacuum sweeper to clean behind the sofa, which is now sitting in the middle of the living room.

The vacuum sweeper hose, as usual, is plugged, so I take it out to the garage to get a stick to clean out the hose. As I'm pushing the stick down the hose all of this birdseed comes falling out, which I now remember plugged up the vacuum when I was cleaning out my car after the birdseed bag broke while I was fixing a muffler clamp. That was an afternoon I'd rather forget.

I decided I had better sweep up the birdseed before I put the vacuum back together to clean behind the sofa, so I could move the speakers to put the entertainment system back together before I got the clamps to fix the drawer, glue the wallpaper, empty the water pail, put in the furnace filter, do the bannister, nail up the picture and fix the stupid squeak.

Unfortunately, I ran out of time and didn't get to do any of that stuff. But, I did get the ladder and change the light bulb over the sink. And my wife thinks I don't do anything around the house.

# Chapter 5
# SURVIVING THE HIGHWAY

*I love to start my day on the road with breakfast served by a waitress with a nose ring, tongue stud and a bad cold. As the song says "life is a highway" and I don't need directions to get where I'm going because I'm a man and every trip I take is an adventure, just like on Wild Kingdom.*

*Scientists have found that men have superior navigational skills, which make them immune from having to stop at 7-Eleven stores for directions.*

# SURVIVING WITHOUT DIRECTIONS

Like most men, I have an unerring sense of direction, which allows me to travel hundreds, even thousands of miles, to the most distant cities without ever consulting a map, road sign or other navigational device.

Once at my destination, all I need is a brief glance at one of those rental car maps that shows the major roads and I can find my way around the most confusing city.

Even though I've displayed this talent for many years, my wife, Madeline, will often insist while I'm driving that I stop and ask directions. This sometimes occurs when we're taking a two-mile trip to Fred and Bubba's Shoppe and Bag, where we go every week.

"Are you sure we're on the right road?" she will ask as we pass familiar landmarks like our mailbox and the big green house at the end of the street that has Christmas decorations up year-round.

"Maybe we should stop and ask directions," she'll suggest as the glow of Fred and Bubba's neon sign comes into view.

Of course, Madeline, like most women, doesn't have the same directional divining skills as men, which we have developed over thousands of years of finding our way back home from the hunt through unmarked forests. In more recent times, men have honed these skills finding their way back home from the sports bar after a night of drinking "sodas" with guys.

Women, on the other hand, feel the necessity to stop and ask directions every 200 yards.

# STOPPING AT 7-ELEVEN

One theory why men and women differ so much on the need for directions is that women require constant input, reassurance and reinforcement that they are on the right track. But instead of listening to the intuitive instincts of their husbands or male friends, women would rather stop and ask directions from total strangers they find lurking at 7-Eleven stores. These are usually people who have trouble remembering what planet they are on, let alone what city they're living in.

Directions from these people usually go like this.

"Well, I'm not sure. I haven't lived here but 10 years and I never leave the store. Maybe Edgar knows. Hey, Edgar, how do you get to watchamacallit street? Oh, wait, now I remember. You go north out of the drive, turn left at the third light, make seven rights until you come to the blue Ford Mustang and then you fall off the edge of whatever planet this is. Waggle Waggle."

It actually makes no difference what they say because neither my wife nor I ever write down the directions given to us. We do this so we can argue later whether it was three lights and then left or seven lights and then three Waggle, Waggles. Sometimes the two of us don't even listen to the directions. Afterward, our conversation sounds like this:

"Well, do you know where to go now?" Madeline asks.

"No, I wasn't paying attention." I reply. " Do you remember anything?"

"I think he said something about turning left somewhere." she'll reply.

"That's enough for me to go on," I respond. "I think I know how to get us there now."

Then I'll wander around aimlessly until I find where we want to go. Of course, the whole time Madeline is insisting we should stop and ask further directions from someone wearing a wet suit, flippers and a kilt.

## "WHERE AM I?"

The other theory of why women have to stop and ask directions is that they never pay any attention to where they are going. A woman just gets in the car and goes on autopilot until she drives long enough and then looks up and asks, "Where am I?" They do this because they are thinking about 10,000 other things besides driving.

Except now, this is not a theory. Scientists have found that men have superior navigational skills, which make them immune from having to stop at 7-Eleven stores for directions.

A Dr. Matthais Riepe of the University of Ulm, which is somewhere off the Autobahn in Germany, tested a dozen men and women and found that men use both sides of their brain to navigate, while women only use one part of their left brain and a smidgen of the frontal lobe that is also used to find malls and shoe stores.

Riepe found that men depend on a banana-shaped guidance system in the brain called a hippocampus. Believe me, I'm not making this up. When I read the words "men," "banana-shaped brain parts" and "hippocampus," I immediately thought "there's a joke in there somewhere." But I couldn't find it.

Scientists believe this fruit-shaped brain sphere in the hippopotamus gives men the confidence and self-esteem to announce they have "arrived" whether it's the right location or not.

In tests, scientists found it took men an average of two minutes to figure out how to get out of a computer maze, while it took women over three minutes to tackle the same course. Men were even faster getting out of the maze if they are told they could skip taking the garbage out and have a beer as a reward at the end.

What the tests found — and this was written up in a scholarly journal not unlike People magazine — is that the difference between men and women traveling a maze is that women have a major handicap. They keep stopping and asking for directions. Waggle Waggle.

94

*When I flipped up "A golfing holiday on championship*
*golf courses" everyone shouted, "What places*
*Dad will never see this summer?"*

# SURVIVING VACATION JEOPARDY

It's July and my family and I are well into our annual game of "Family Vacation Jeopardy."

Unlike the real television Jeopardy game, where contestants compete for money and the prestigious title "Jeopardy Champion and keeper of little-known facts that are useless in the real world," with Family Vacation Jeopardy we compete to find a week during the summer when the five of us can get together and go someplace fun as a family that doesn't cost too much.

Categories in the first round of Family Vacation Jeopardy:

*"Times that are out for me"*
*"I think I'm free ...."*
*"We have company here the week of ..."*
*"What I can reschedule"*
*"Oh, wait. I forgot about ..."*

The first round starts in May, when we eliminated all of June, most of July and the later half of August, finally ending the round with 5 and 1/4 days we can spend together in August if Aunt Martha doesn't show up.

## JEOPARDY ROUND TWO

We usually get to the second round of 'Vacation Jeopardy' in June. During this part of the game, we define where we want to go and what we want to do. This is a very tough round and requires all the skill the parent contestants can muster to keep from having to spend most of a week doing strange and dangerous things the kids think are great fun.

For example, when the category "Where to go/do?" is flipped, and the card, "Visit Tupelo, Miss. Search for Elvis guitar picks in the backwoods," pops up, the correct response from my wife and I was, "What would Elvis not want us to do on our vacation?"

Likewise, when our outdoor adventuresome son turned up the answer, "Mountain climbing Pike's Peak and white water rafting the Snake River," our answer, of course, was, "What will injure your parents, raise their health insurance and cause them physical pain?"

This is not a one-sided game. The boys also get their turns. So, when the Family Vacation Jeopardy board for "Places to go/do?" popped up with, "A tour of cozy bed and breakfast hotels of the Northeast" the boys answered in unison, "What tour will you not see us on this summer?"

Likewise when I flipped up, "A golfing holiday on championship golf courses" everyone shouted, "What places Dad will never see this summer?"

This week, we start the final Jeopardy round in which costs are determined. I already know my wife, Madeline, will be out there saying, "I'll take vacations for $2,000, Alex," while I'm hoping to get a shot at "Vacations for $400."

## VACATION IN THE 1950s

We didn't have to play this game when I was growing up in the 1950s. We knew when my father's vacation was going to be a year or more in advance because his plant always shut down the first two weeks in July.

My brother and I never got a chance to voice where we'd like to go. My parents always picked the spot and it was always somewhere a thousand miles away that required driving at 10 mph on two-lane roads that were under construction for 900 miles.

I'll tell you right now, the vacation spots my parents picked never had a) amusement parks, b) cities nearby, c) movie theaters, d) running water. The destinations always had wonderful sounding names like "Lake of the Ozark," "The Finger Lakes

Region" and "Thousand Islands," but no matter where we went we always wound up staying at the same mosquito-infested campground named "Slackjaw-Achers," living in a lean-to tent or "Rustic Cabin."

The tents always leaked and the cabins were usually constructed out of discarded piano crates someone remodeled into "family suites" that offered two double beds, a dresser and a bath in so little space you had to walk on the beds to cross the room and stand on the dresser to get into the bath.

We'd spend the next 10 days there with Mom cooking on an outside grill and Dad playing golf while my brother and I shot black flies off each other with rubber band guns — the same stuff we would have been doing at home without the 1000-mile trek.

Our alternate family vacation in those days was the 2,000 mile road trip, where we saw 37 states in 10 days riding in a car without air conditioning in 95 degree heat. Most of the trip, my brother and I would sleep in the back seat, rising only once-in-a-while to hit each other.

## TRAVELING WITH DAD

Sometimes, my dad called out some famous landmark we should see. He'd go, "Wake up, there's Mount Rushmore" or "Wow, Old Faithful is erupting," or "Look quick, you'll miss the Grand Canyon." He'd usually say these things all in the same day because we never stopped for anything once the car started.

Food, drinks and an empty milk jug for convenience were our constant companions on these trips. Our only objective was to see how far we could travel in a day. "I'd like to get to Albuquerque by nightfall," Dad would say as we pulled out of Chicago at 6 a.m. "We'll stop there for the night and then head east to Florida for the Sponge Festival."

I tried to do one of these road trips once with my family. I had all our clothes plus food, drinks and an empty milk jug packed up and in the car by 7 a.m. while the rest of the family hadn't yet stuffed a sock in a bag.

We finally started out at nine, but with return trips for forgotten clothes, bathroom breaks and pit stops to stretch our legs, we only got to the end of the drive by noon, so we stopped for a picnic lunch.

By nightfall, we had reached the edge of town, where we took a room. We wound up staying the week shooting black flies off each other with rubber band guns. After that, we invented Family Vacation Jeopardy and have been much happier.

*I find there's nothing more appetizing to start your day on the road than to sit down at a restaurant for breakfast and be served by a waitress with a nose ring and tongue stud.*

# SURVIVING ROAD TRIPS

There's nothing like getting away from the pressures of the world for a few days and going on a road trip. It doesn't matter where you go—north, south, east or west—it's the adventure of the trip that counts. I recently took a road trip, and these are some of the observations I made along the way.

Two things always happen on road trips. About a half-hour from home, I start to wonder if I shut the coffee pot off. The other thing that always happens is about two hours into the trip, my perfectly running car starts making funny noises in the engine. "Was that knock there before? What's that rattle?"

Whenever I stop at turnpike rest areas, I always look for people I know in the crowds, but never see anyone I recognize. I'm sure that during any given stop, there are people I know, or people who know other people we both know. They should have a big chalkboard when you enter where you can mark down your name and the town where you live. "Mike Smith, South Bend, Ind. Will take greetings and messages for friends at table six."

On the road, do you ever wonder where people in moving vans are going? And why they're leaving? Were they run out of town? Will they have a better life somewhere else, or more of the same with different scenery?

## MEALS AND WHEELS

I find there's nothing more appetizing to start your day on the road than to sit down at a restaurant for breakfast and be served by a waitress with a nose ring and tongue stud. It's even more inviting if the waitress has a head cold and keeps blowing little bubbles out of the hole of the nose ring when she talks. "Wud ya like coffee wid your breakfast? (pop)"

Did you ever notice that at truckers' restaurants, there is no such thing as a diet meal on the menu. Everything is fried, deep fried or battered and deep fried. And it's served with gravy.

At one truck stop restaurant, I ordered the "Vegetarian Vegetable Surprise." The surprise part was the vegetables came battered and deep fried with gravy on the side.

Another thing I don't understand is why restaurants serve lettuce and cabbage leaves with bacon and eggs? I've never seen anyone take a cabbage leaf or piece of lettuce and dip it in their eggs. What's even worse is when they put orange slices on top your eggs. If I wanted the taste of an orange on my eggs I'd pour orange juice over them. And parsley. No one eats parsley, yet it's on the side of every dinner plate. Does anyone ever cry, "I didn't get parsley with my breaded, deep fried chicken steak covered in gravy."

## TRUCK DRIVIN' MAN

Truck stops are the most fascinating places in the world. Where else could you find a gift shop that offers both a hand-crafted "Elvis" rug and an 8-foot-long chrome truck muffler hanging next to each other.

Until this trip, I used to have the perception that truck drivers are all hard-boiled, tough characters with a penchant for jeans, T-shirts, motorcycle boots and cholesterol plus diets. Well, most of that's true. But at one truck stop, I watched this big burly trucker looking at a display of ceramic items. He spent a good five minutes looking at each item, gently picking them up and putting them down before he made his selection and went to the cash register.

When he was gone, I walked over to the display to see what he had selected. To my surprise it was a delicate ceramic casting of a mouse family having tea in the drawing room. That driver may have looked like he could bench press diesel engines, but he had a marshmallow for a heart.

On the other hand, I stopped by the video game room at the same truck stop and watched another trucker playing a game called "Death Race" on one of the machines. The object of the game was to win the race at the highest speed you could attain while running other vehicles off the road. I watched him smash up dozens of cars before I decided I better get back on the road before he did. I wanted to be out there in front of him.

One final thought on truck drivers. Do they all talk with a southern accent? Is this a job requirement in the trucking profession? Or, is it a cultural thing, like all airline pilots have to sound like they've gone to the Chuck Yeager school of annunciation? I wonder if Canadian truck drivers also sound as if they are from the South?

## TURNPIKE TRAVEL WONDERS

Did you know the Turnpike through Northern Indiana is so flat and straight you can drive and read a book. It's so flat you can see for miles ahead of you. You can just tuck the book between the steering wheel, read a few pages, look up, correct your course out of the corn field back to the road, and continue reading. It's probably the only place in the world I'd allow myself to drive and use a cellular phone at the same time.

You see a lot of police cars on the highway when you're traveling, and most of them are racing by you at 90 mph. I got to wondering, are police cruisers allowed to exceed the speed limit when they're not chasing anyone? And what excuse would they have for doing it? They're already at work, so they can't claim they're rushing to get to work because they're late. Or, are they speeding so they can get into position to catch someone else speeding? Does two wrongs make them right?

Has anyone ever gotten one of those $29.95 rooms that are advertised on the highway? I had never come across one of those rooms in my life until this trip. My advice, after staying in one, is go the extra 10 bucks and get a real room.

I've noticed that the dirtiest restrooms on the road always have signs in them that say, "Please notify management if this restroom needs cleaning." I went into one restroom at a convenience store that had such a sign and the restroom was absolutely filthy. So, I went and told the clerk behind the counter about the dirty restroom. He gave me a bucket and mop and some Windex.

And finally, the one thing I learned most about being on the highway. The drive home always takes longer than the ride going out.

*Vacation journal entry: "Forgot to put our collie Jo in the kennel. Can't get the smell of wet dog off us. Will write more when we find the tent that just blew away in the storm."*

# SURVIVING THE FAMILY VACATION

It's summer. The weather is lousy. Gas prices are above $2 a gallon. So obviously, it's time to go on the annual family summer vacation.

I don't know about you, but I've always looked on summer vacations as a time of wonder — as in "I wonder why we went?" I can usually accurately predict our vacation will be a disaster each year.

For one thing, our vacations always involve lots of water even though we almost never go to the beach. The water is usually in the form of rain, hail, sleet, tornadoes, hurricanes and on alternate years, flooding.

But getting away from it all for a week with the family makes it all worth while. To go on a one-week vacation, though, it usually takes us three weeks to get ready. First of all, we have to cancel all the dental appointments, athletic events, dinner engagements and miscellaneous home product demonstrations we mistakenly made that coincide with our annual trip. That usually takes three days.

The rest of the time is spent packing. You see, when we go on trips, we don't actually leave home. We just put everything we own into the car and take it with us. On one trip, we packed so much stuff we had to go out and buy a cargo van so we could actually have room for the children.

But, after weeks of preparation for the trip, there's nothing quite as satisfying as piling in the car, camper, van or U-Haul truck and getting on the road. Usually, our first stop of the trip is at the end of the driveway, at which point someone calls out "potty break" and another one asks, "Are we there yet?"

# DO NOT PASS GO

That's usually my cue to say, "I can't believe we have to stop already. We just left the house." But, I'm always coaxed into going back to the house at this point because:

a) we've left someone behind, probably our son Matt who is sound asleep in the garage
b) we've forgotten to turn off some major electrical appliance like a table saw
c) the dog is sitting in the drive waving goodbye to us instead of being in the kennel where we forgot to put her
d) school has started again.

Over the years, our family has taken a variety of vacations to any number of interesting places. I've kept a journal of the jaunts and I would like to highlight some excerpts from my vacation journals for you.

*July, something (date washed away by rainwater), 1982.*
We've gone on our first family camping trip. So far, it's rained all week. Kids are complaining about lack of electricity for televisions, VCR, computer, video games, stereo system and microwave they've brought with them.

Forgot to put our collie Jo in the kennel again. Can't get the smell of wet dog off us. Will write more when we find the tent that just blew away in the storm.

*June something, something, vacation trip to the seashore.*
Bright sunny weather all the way to Myrtle Beach. Spent this afternoon on the beach getting sun until the hurricane rolled in. North Carolina governor has evacuated the coast.

*(Same trip, sometime later.)*
Spent the last five days at a tacky amusement park called "South of the Border" with 650 other refugee tourists looking for

something to do. Have sustained ourselves eating bean burritos for all three meals. Entertainment is trying to toss waterlogged softballs into sombreros.

*April (date and year totally obliterated by water)*

We've gone off to Mammoth Caves, Ky., to explore the grandeur of these underground natural wonders. As usual for our vacation, it is raining, but for once we're underground most of the day, so who cares.

A forest ranger tour guide takes us on enthralling walk through the wondrous caverns. Whenever the forest ranger stops for questions, our son Jason asks "Does Batman live here?" He asks the question 47 times, alternating it with "Where's Robin?"

Matthew disappears during the tour. After an hour search, we find him sleeping in one of the tunnels. Nathan pretends to fall down a "bottomless sinkhole" for laughs. We become the first family ever banned from Mammoth Caves.

Rest of trip washed out by flooding.

*"J" something and a "1" still visible.*

Took family on fishing trip. Rained buckets. Fish drowned.

*August, something with a "7" or "2" at the end, 1992*

Went on a road trip to national historic sights on east coast. Plan to see Gettysburg, Washington, D.C., and someplace where everyone wears colonial clothes and build things by hand, and Busch Gardens.

We drove all night because Nathan has his license and we have three drivers. Nate took the midnight to 3 a.m. shift on the Pennsylvania Turnpike while we slept in the back of the van.

Woke up about 2 a.m. to the sound of tires squalling and Nathan shouting, "Oh, my God, we're going to die," as the van swerves back and forth on two wheels.

"What's happening?" I scream.

He laughs. "Nothing. Go back to sleep."

I don't sleep the rest of the trip.

*July, 14-20, 1999*

Have come to Disney World in Orlando. Experienced no earthquakes or tidal waves along the way. Weather is beautiful here. Found free passes to the park and there are almost no crowds today. Everyone enjoying themselves thoroughly. I think I've come with the wrong family.

*Packing more clothes than one person could wear in a year for a couple days on the road started when I got married.*

# SURVIVING PACKING FOR A TRIP

I've been getting ready to go away on a three day trip. So, of course, I've been packing now for two weeks.

You might ask, how much clothing does one person need to have for a three day trip? So far, I've emptied everything out of my closet, four sets of drawers, two garment storage bags and rummaged through a pile of clothes destined for the Salvation Army to pack for this trip.

Right now, I've whittled my clothing selection down to two steamer trunks and a carry on suitcase the size of a Ford Explorer. I don't know when this problem with packing started. I can remember back in my college days when to get ready for a week- long, cross-country trip I would simply pick out my cleanest jeans and a few sweat shirts that passed the sniff test and I'd be long gone.

In those days, I didn't wear socks, owned one pair of shoes and kept a Grateful Dead tee-shirt in the closet for special occasions. Underwear was worn when it was clean, which is to say mostly after trips home to visit my parents and their free-use washer and drier.

Now, not only do I wear socks, but I even color coordinate them to my pants, shirt, shoes and the color of my underwear. As you can see, packing for me has become a major chore.

## IT STARTED WITH MARRIAGE

Packing more clothes than one person could wear in a year for a couple days on the road began when I got married.

I can remember the first trip I took with my wife, Madeline, after we were first married. It was our honeymoon.

She was taking five suit cases and four small valises of varying sizes. I had packed a gym bag with a pair of jeans and

107

two sweatshirts that had passed the sniff test. Oh, and I had three pairs of brand new white cotton Jockey briefs and a pair of paisley pajamas my mom had bought me for special occasions.

"Is that all you're taking?" Madeline asked, looking at my lonely single bag beside her suitcases.

"We're only going to be gone a week," I said, wondering if the extra sweatshirt was really necessary.

## DRESSING FOR DINNER

"What are you going to wear when we go out to dinner?" she asked.

"Ah, jeans and a sweatshirt?" I queried.

"You're going to need at least a couple dress shirts and a good pair of slacks," she said, starting a pile of necessary honeymoon clothes on the dresser.

"And, if we go to a nice restaurant, you'll need a tie," my new wife suggested, putting three ties of varying hues on the pile for me.

"Why do I need three ties?" I asked.

"In case you spill something on one, you'll have two more for back up," she explained.

"And you're going to need a sports coat. Most nice restaurants require a sports coat," she said.

"But we're going to a cabin in the wilds of Vermont," I protested. "The only thing we're likely to see with coats on out there are bears, and I don't think they'll mind if I'm in jeans and a sweatshirt."

"It doesn't matter, you should always pack for the unexpected, then when it happens, you'll be ready," Madeline explained. "Now that I think of it, you better take a suit in case we go to a really nice restaurant."

Putting that on the pile, she surveyed me up and down and asked, "How many pairs of shoes are you taking?"

I looked down at my Converse sneakers and shrugged my shoulders.

"One?"

108

She shook her head sadly.

"You'll need at least one brown pair and one black pair of dress shoes," she said putting those on the ever growing pile of clothes. "I think you better take some extra dress pants to coordinate with the shoes. Plus, it would be good to have a casual pair of slacks and some loafers," she said, adding those to the pile.

"Now, if the weather turns warm do you have any shorts to wear?" she asked.

"No," I confessed. "But, I can always hack the legs off these jeans and make some cutoffs. Or, if it's a hot day and we're going to a nice restaurant in the woods, I'll just put some vent slits in my suit pants."

She pouted.

"What's the matter?" I asked.

"I'm trying to give you some tips on packing for a trip and you're making fun of me," she said, looking very sad.

"I'm sorry. I didn't mean it. Here, I'll put another suit on the pile," I said trying to console her.

She smiled at me and took the suit I'd laid on the pile and put it back in the closet.

"You don't look good in that gray suit. We'll take the brown one," she said, putting the brown suit on the pile.

"I almost forgot. I bought you some new socks for the trip. I think 14 pairs should be enough, don't you?" she said, arranging a huge stack of socks on the dresser.

"And now, what do you have if it turns cold out there?"

In all, I ended up taking my gym bag plus three suitcases of clothes on our honeymoon. As it turned out, I don't remember having to even unpack the gym bag.

Times change, though, and these days when I travel I usually take with me three-quarters of all the apparel I own. The really sad part is that no matter how much I take, I always need something I left behind.

*"We've got to hurry. Thanksgiving dinner is at noon and it's a four hour trip," I'd announce, often doing a little dance of impatience to show the urgency for speed.*

# SURVIVING THANKSGIVING TRAVEL

This weekend will mark the start of the annual pilgrimage across the United States of people heading home for the Thanksgiving weekend with family and friends.

Oh, how I remember those days, packing up the car, the three kids, the dog and a half-ton of baby accessories for the four hour trip through holiday traffic to Grandma and Grandpa's house.

The trips all started the same way. We'd plan to be up at 6 a.m. and be on the road by 7:30 a.m. It would always turn out that this would be the one day of the year everybody slept in, so that instead of being packed and ready to go by 7:30, we'd be just waking up at that time.

I'd jump out of bed and start rushing around like crazy, throwing everything into the car I could lay my hands on, often packing dirty laundry and bird seed in the trunk along with our suitcases and clothes. While I was moving at the speed of light to make up lost time, the rest of the family would be moving in slow motion, often stopping to read a book, take leisurely showers or stare blankly off into space.

"We've got to hurry. Thanksgiving dinner is at noon and it's a four hour trip," I'd announce, often doing a little dance of impatience to show the urgency for speed. It never did any good. Everybody would just say they were hurrying and then go back to whatever they were doing, which usually had nothing to do with getting ready for the Thanksgiving trip.

Eventually, one-by-one, everyone would come out of the house and get in the car and we'd pull out to the end of the driveway where we'd make our first stop.

"Where's Matt?" my wife, Madeline, would ask. We'd do a nose count and, more times than not, discover we were one nose short. So we'd go back into the house and rouse Matt from his bed and direct him to the car.

Matt has always, since a baby, been the epitome of energy conservation. The night before a vacation he puts on all the clothes he's going to wear on the trip and goes to bed in them. He sleeps until everyone is in the car ready to go, then he staggers - eyes shut - to the back seat, and promptly falls back to sleep for the rest of the trip, waking only partially, now and again, to take food and liquids.

## GOING NO WHERE FAST

On most trips, Matt could easily have stayed in bed for another hour, because we would usually make a half dozen return trips to the house to get things we forgot before getting on the road. During the start of one Thanksgiving trip, we actually put on more miles backing in and out of the driveway than we did on the highway to their grandparents.

Somewhere around nine o'clock, the trip would begin.

About 15 seconds down the road from our house, our son Jason would announce, "Let's go to breakfast. I'm hungry." Another 30 seconds later he would cry, "I'm starving." So within five minutes of leaving home, we would be stopped in line at the McDonald's drive-through behind 30 other cars, full of families like us, trying since dawn to get on the road.

After McDonald's, we'd get a good 5 to 6 miles on the highway before the first potty break. "All right," I'd announce as everyone got out of the car. "We'll meet back here in five minutes and be on the road." I could just as easily have announced, "We have reached our destination and will be staying at the Sunoco convenience shop through Christmas."

In five minutes, I would be back at the car ready to go and everyone else — except Matt, who was still sleeping— would be no where in sight.

Back I'd go into the store to track them down. The boys would be playing video games, while my wife browsed for Christmas gifts. Rounding everyone up, we'd pay for our purchases, get back in the car and go another five miles, at which point Matt would wake up and say, "I thought we were stopping to go to the bathroom," and we'd have to repeat the process over again.

## SHOES TAKE A WALK

And that would be how the whole trip would go, with us stopping every few miles to checkout the facilities of every rest area, convenience store and service centers on the highway.

Every once in a while, we'd get up a head of steam and put maybe 30 miles or so on the road without stopping. Then someone would shout "Dad, Jason threw his shoes out the window." I'd look back and, sure enough, there would be a pair of shoes bouncing along the highway.

"Why'd you do that?" I'd demand, turning the car around to fetch the shoes. "Nathan made me do it," he'd say.

"How'd he make you do it?" I'd query and Jay would reply "He looked at me."

So I'd reprimand Jason to stop throwing his shoes out the window, and Nathan to stop looking at him, and we'd be off again for another quarter mile until Jay would announce "these aren't my shoes."

Eventually, we'd get to the folks' home and my mother would welcome us by saying, "We thought you'd never get here. You should try getting an earlier start next time."

# Chapter 6
# SURVIVING CHILDHOOD

*Childhood is a wonderful magical time, full of the fun and
excitement of learning things like phonics and spelling so you
can read Playboy and other great literature.  That is if you can
first survive the hazards of evolution, stupid kid tricks and
things the Three Stooges taught you. Nyuk, Nyuk, Nyuk, Nyuk.*

*On the opening day of school, the teacher would decide who had potential to graduate and become a productive member of society and which of us were going to be hoboes.*

# SURVIVING PHONICS

Phonics has been used in this country for generations to teach little kids how to read by making them sound out words phonetically, as in "reedin iss ez wit fonix."

According to history, phonics was developed during the third century B.C. by the Phoenicians who used it as a military weapon to drive their enemies crazy. It still has that effect today if you ask any first-grader who has to learn to read using the system and its thousands of rules and exceptions.

Teacher: "Jimmy, just remember that the letters 'g' and 'h' when together sound like an 'f' as in the word 'rough' but are silent when together in words like 'dough,' but can also sometimes sound like a 'g' when together in the word 'ghost.'

"Is that clear?"

A new system called 'Whole language learning' on the other hand is based on a philosophy that says, "Give them something interesting and fun to read and they'll learn in spite of themselves."

Educators have decided the two opposing systems should be combined because nearly 40 percent of U.S. elementary school kids can't read today. And it's my guess it's because of phonics. The following is a true story about how I learned to read using the two different systems. At the end, you can make up your mind which one is better.

Like many people, I am the product of learning to read and spell through the use of phonics. Now, you don't know it but I had to translate that last sentence from phonics to English in my head before I put it down on paper. In its original form it read "Like meny people, I am da produkt of lerning 2 rede and rite thru da uze of fonix." Scary isn't it.

# REEDIN' ISSNT EZ

All I could think of when I was introduced to phonics in the first grade was, "This would be a good time to go back to kindergarten, crawl under a blanket and take a nap."

Back when I was learning to read, the teaching system they used was fairly simple. Everybody started out evenly in the first grade and the teacher on the opening day of school simply decided who had potential to graduate and become a productive member of society and which of us were going to be hoboes. They did this based on your ability to read that famous first learning manual "Dick and Jane fail you out of Harvard." The book consisted of simple sentences like "See Dick. See Dick run. Run, Dick, run."

When it came my turn to read, it came out: " S e e e e . . . e e e e . . . e e e e . . . e e e e Daaaaaaaa.....iiiiiiiiiiii........ccccccc......kkkkkkkkkk . Seeee...eeee...eeee...eeee Daaaaaaaa.....iiiiiiiiiiii....." That's about as far as I got when the teacher decided it was time to put us into reading groups. I waited for my name to be called as the teacher picked the best readers to be "Bluebirds" and I waited while she picked the members of the "Robins" and then the "Larks."

I eventually wound up in the reading group called the "Snipes" which was one level below "Cowbirds" and two away from "Grackles." My group consisted of me and a boy named Edgar who stuttered so bad when he tried to read, it sounded like Morse Code.

I'll never forget how alone I felt the day they moved Edgar up to the "Cowbird" reading group and I was the only "Snipe" left. The teacher did this to set an example and give us all incentive to try to read better, so one day we could be Robins or even Bluebirds. I never even made it to "Grackle." By the second grade, they were going to keep me back a year because my reading was so bad, and my phonics-assisted spelling was "inkombrehesable."

I only made it into the second grade by memorizing the words in the book "Dick and Jane" and pretending to read them, which was pretty hilarious because I finished reading the book and was still only on page three.

## LIVING IN PHONICS HELL

I might have been condemned to a "phonics hell" the rest of my life if it hadn't been for a kindly third grade teacher who one day asked me why I couldn't read. I said it was because there was nothing interesting in the books. And so she asked me what I was interested in and I said, "Space and rockets," which was a big thing back then.

So she (all elementary teachers were women in those days, especially in my school because they were also all nuns) opened the drawer where teachers kept all their confiscated things like water guns and bubble gum, and pulled out a science fiction book by Robert Heinlein titled "The Green Hills of Earth." She handed it to me saying, "Here. Go read this and come back when you're done." She didn't bother me after that about reading as long as I had that science fiction book with me.

Well, I've got to say during the first part of the book, which were all short stories about people in space, I could read and comprehend about every seventh word. By the middle of the book I was up to one out of five words and by the end the book one out of three words made sense to me. So I read the book again, and all of a sudden the words had meaning and this whole world of space and adventure and human heroics opened up to me and I was hooked on reading — as opposed to being "Hooked on phonics," which is a gag gift for parents who want to make their kids miserable at home in their spare time.

It took me three months to read the book twice and when I was done, I proudly put it back on the teacher's desk and announced "I finished reading it " to which she said, "That's wonderful, now write me a book report on it."

So I did, and the report went something like this: " I likt dis bouk vary mooch. It waz xsiding." Although I went on to become an excellent reader, it took me another 12 years to learn how to translate phonics spelling into real English.

*What I really wanted was a book bag with Roy Rogers and Trigger on it. My friend, Vince, had one, and I envied him. Can you believe I once had book bag envy?*

## SURVIVING SCHOOL DAYS

For the past month or so, I've been kind of "antsy." I feel like I should be doing something  important and I can't quite figure out what it is. Well, the other day it finally dawned on me what I should be doing. It's September and I should be going back to school.

Now, I haven't been a student since before disco hit. But every September, my mind subconsciously reminds me it's time for a new school year. For weeks before Labor Day, I have these uncontrollable urges to buy yellow No. 2 pencils, find my three-ring binder with subject dividers and get some new school clothes. Except, I couldn't figure out why the urges were occurring and thought I was going crazy when I'd find myself wandering around stationery stores gazing longingly at lined yellow note pads.

I still remember the thrill of being back in school each year, seeing old friends and finding out what they did on their summer vacations. Wondering if there would be any new girls in my classes. What teachers I was going to have. Which ones I wasn't going to like. What subjects I might fail.

Back in grade school, the teachers would hand out our new books and then have us make jacket covers for them out of brown paper bags. On the covers, we were told to print, as neatly as we could, the name of the subject, our names, grades and the school we went to so in case we left them on the playground, they would be returned to us.

You could always tell the girls' books from the guys' books in my school by the covers. The girls in my class would decorate their covers with flowers and puppies and pretty pictures. The guys would always draw monsters, hot rods and jet airplanes.

The teachers in my elementary school would hold a cover

contest for the best cover design. The girls' book covers always won for some reason, no matter how great the monsters were that we guys drew.

## BOOK BAG ENVY

It's funny the things you remember about school. What I remember most about elementary school is book bags. Book bags were the things you carried your monster-covered books in before someone invented backpacks.

My book bag was green with brown plastic trim and a picture of a little red schoolhouse on it.

I hated that bag. I drew pictures on the schoolhouse of monsters coming out of the windows and flames roaring out of the bell tower. If I were a kid today and did that, they'd put me into a little padded room for observation. What I really wanted was a book bag with Roy Rogers and Trigger on it. My friend, Vince, had one, and I envied him. Can you believe I once had book bag envy?

We left our book bags behind when we went to junior high. It wasn't cool to have a book bag there. So we carried our books "au natural" in our hands or jauntily tucked between our right arm and hip. Except for Vince. He still carried his Roy Rogers book bag, but no one envied him anymore.

Junior high, or what they now call middle school, brought a major change in me. Dion was the singing idol and Chubby Checker was doing the Twist and I showed up with my hair slicked back with Brylcream. I had a DA in back and a wave in front that dipped half way down my forehead. I made the "Fonz" look like an upright citizen. The girls loved it. Within two months, every guy in school was wearing his hair the same way. I didn't do too much studying during that stage. I was too busy combing my hair.

Unlike most people, I don't remember too much about high school. The only thing I remember is that all the girls wore miniskirts, which is probably the reason I don't remember much else about high school.

# BEEHIVE ENVY

I do remember the beehive hair styles the girls wore. There seemed to be a rule in our school that the shorter the miniskirt worn, the taller the beehive had to be. Renee had the tallest beehive in the school. She had to duck when she entered doorways. Almost all the girls envied her. Her hair was the high school equivalent of Vince's book bag.

The girls who didn't have beehives wore their hair long and straight and even ironed it to get that Joan Baez folk singer look. The rule of thumb here was the longer the straight hair, the shorter the mini skirt.

Unlike elementary school and middle school, which seemed to go on forever, high school was over in about 10 minutes. One day, I was a lowly freshman, lost in this gigantic school, and the next day I was graduating.

I found at that point I had a choice to make. I could go to work in the mill and become a responsible member of the community, or I could go off to college for four more years of education and extend my childhood.

I chose college. It was the right decision. College was even better than high school because no one made you go to class if you didn't want to and you could stay up all night playing Euchre, a card game invented by college students to fill the time when they are supposed to be studying. In college, I majored in Euchre with a minor in Hearts.

Those days are gone. Now that I am older and wiser, I look back on my 16 years of formal education and I have only one regret. I still wish I had gotten that Roy Rogers and Trigger book bag. I saw one in an antique catalog the other day and it was worth $1,800. How I wish I had that bag.

*Evolution just never comes up in conversation. Once in a while, my tax account might ask, "Do you believe we have evolved from lower primates?" and I'll go, "Only if it reduces my federal withholding taxes."*

## SURVIVING EVOLUTION

The state Board of Education in Kansas, in a peevish mood because federal courts won't allow the teaching of creationism in schools, has struck back by banning the teaching of evolution in state schools.

For those of you who are unfamiliar with the debate over evolution versus creationism, I'm not going to bother explaining it because it's too complicated and probably violates some Kansas law. And besides, you probably don't care anyway.

But this issue has been a major concern for many people in many parts of the country, most of whom have never actually been to Kansas.

While people across the United States are taking sides as to whether the Kansas decision is "backwardism" or a major win for biblical true believers, high school kids all over the state of Kansas are cheering the Board of Education decision.

The kids are going, "Wow, that's 50 million years worth of junk we don't have to study." Of course, not all of them are saying that. The Bible-raised kids are going, "Whoopee, that's 6,000 years of junk we won't have on the next test. Now, we'll have more time to play 'Tomb Raider XVII.'"

I feel sorry for these kids. They will now never have the chance to even get a rudimentary grasp of how this world began because they won't be able to study evolution or learn about the earth's history like I did in school. They'll go through life not knowing that the Jurassic Park period preceded the Croatian period or that penguins invented the tuxedo down in the Galapagos Island, to attend formal cocktail parties Darwin threw for them.

## EVOLUTION AND KFC

Who, am I kidding? I don't remember anything I studied in high school about evolution, and if the truth be known, I haven't had a serious discussion on the subject in the past 30 years. Evolution just never comes up in conversation. Once in a while my tax account might ask, "Do you believe we have evolved from lower primates?" and I'll go, "Only if it reduces my federal withholding taxes or affects my FICA benefits."

I mean no one in my life talks Darwin or the theory of evolution. My auto mechanic never brings it up. The guys I play golf with don't discuss it. Even the ones who hit the golf ball like gorillas don't care. Evolution never appears on my bank statements or utility bills. And in all the years I watched the Cubs play baseball, I only heard Harry Carey once yell, "Well, I'm a monkey's uncle; he caught that liner backhanded."

The only place I suspect evolution may be impacting my life is on my telephone bills from the phone company. I haven't deciphered all of their billing codes yet, but I'm beginning to believe Ameritech has a charge in there somewhere for evolution, because they darn well charge me for everything else on this planet.

The only time evolution ever came up for me was once in college. A roommate and I were devouring a bucket of KFC chicken over the evening newspaper when he came across a picture of some scientist holding up a bone, declaring it was the missing link that proved man evolved from lower forms of life. My roommate looked at the bone in the picture and then set down a chicken bone next to it and declared, "Look, it's the same bone. We're descended from chickens. I wonder if Colonel Sanders knows this."

## BILLY'S A MONKEY

Actually, the people in Kansas really had nothing to worry about in the teaching of evolution in school because I've been there and I can tell you exactly what happens in a school room when evolution comes up. It goes like this.

Teacher: "... and Darwin's theory of evolution postulates that over millions of years of natural selection, moving from the single cell amoeba to more complex ..."

This lecture goes on for about two days, and finally, at the end of the lecture—that all of the students slept through—the instructor finally says:

"... and humans likely developed from lower primates such as the monkey."

Everyone in the classroom at that point starts laughing and one kids stands up and yells, "Billy's a monkey," at which point Billy jumps on a desk and scratches himself under the arms making Cheetah noises until the teacher makes all of us pull out pencils and paper and write a thousand times, "I will not make fun of evolution."

Then, a week later, when the question "explain evolution" comes up on the test half the kids in the class will leave the answer blank, while the rest write down "Billy is a monkey."

That's the way they taught evolution in my school, by gosh, and if it was good enough for me, then it should be good enough for students in Kansas. They have a right to know Billy's a monkey and we all evolved from chicken bones.

*As one who watched the Three Stooges for many years, I've managed to grow up to be a contributing member of society — "Nyuk, Nyuk, Nyuk, Nyuk."*

# SURVIVING EARLY ROLE MODELS

The newspapers recently have been full of stories about how professional wrestling — that amalgamation of choreographed mayhem, soap opera and larger-than-life villains and heroes — is causing children to hurt each other while practicing "body slams," "clotheslines" and "pile drivers" on their friends and siblings.

As a responsible, mature adult who recently got "head butted" by a five-year-old aspiring wrestler, I am "concerned" about the sport. Being a responsible journalist, I feel the need to speak out about this.

On the other hand, there are people out there in this sport with names like "The Rock," "Maniac" and the "Grim Reaper," who all weight 400 pounds and can pop my head off like a Brussels sprout, so I'll just say that I am "concerned" and let them draw their own conclusions.

Actually, what is being reported about wrestling today is the exact same stuff they were saying about my television heroes, "The Three Stooges," back in the 1950s. Parents and media critics back then attacked Larry, Curly and Moe as violent, juvenile Neanderthals who taught children how to hit each other in the head with hammers, poke out eyes, pull people around by the nose with pliers and generally hurt each other.

As one who watched the Stooges for many years, I've managed to grow up to be a contributing member of society — "Nyuk, Nyuk, Nyuk, Nyuk" — without once starting a pie fight at a high-class social event. (All right, maybe I did it once, but it needed to be done.)

I have to say I have had no ill affect from watching these maniacs — "Whoop, whoop, whoop, whoop."

In fact, if there's anyone out there that says I have been affected, just let me know and I'll gouge their eyes out.

Rather than warp me, the Three Stooges taught me many valuable lessons about life, most of which I still live by today. And I'd like to take this opportunity to share them with you, you knuckleheads.

## STOOGES RULES OF LIFE

1. The Three Stooges showed me that even if you fight with your friends, they are still your friends.

2. Moe taught me there is always someone out there who wants to belt you in the head if they don't get their way.

3. Curly proved that timing is everything, especially if you are trying to avoid an eye gouge.

4. Larry demonstrated that even grown-ups can have bad hair days.

5. The Stooges proved you can make a living at anything, even being silly, if you are good at it.

6. Curly taught me to never mess with people who slap their heads when they get mad.

7. From the Stooges, we all learned that some people can take even the most innocent situations and turn them into a pie fight.

8. And the boys taught us to never hire wallpaper hangers who advertise themselves as "The Three Stooges."

9. I also learned from the Stooges never to mention "Niagara Falls" to Schemp Howard.

10. Moe proved to be an excellent example that the "brains" of the outfit aren't always as smart as they think.

11. Larry, Curly and Moe demonstrated that some people naturally attract trouble.

12. And rude manners are contagious.

13. I discovered from Curly that when things look down, a simple "Nyuk, Nyuk, Nyuk, Nyuk" can brighten my day.

14. And who among us didn't learn from watching the Stooges that even the most serious and pompous occasions can have their funny moments.

15. The Stooges taught us kids that we shouldn't emulate everything adults do.

16. I learned that "knucklehead" can be an affectionate term.

17. I also learned there's no defense against a closed-fist, windmill-windup head bonk.

18. And, I've discovered that the "Curly Shuffle" gets harder to do the older you get.

19. Finally, the most important thing I learned about life from these guys is that no matter how tough things are, the Three Stooges never solved their problems with guns.

*I was 18 and I could still claim to be the only person in the*
*country who actually did read Playboy for the articles.*
*Go ahead, just ask me how to properly tie an ascot.*

# SURVIVING MEMORIES OF PLAYBOY

It just goes to prove if you live long enough, anybody can become an elder statesmen.

Last week, the Chicago City Council dedicated a street corner on Michigan Avenue "Hugh Hefner Way" after the founder of "Playboy" magazine, once this country's leading nudie picture book.

There with the article was a picture of good old — and I do mean old — Hugh Hefner, standing on his street corner with two beautiful blondes on his arm.

I found the picture of "Hef" with those two beautiful young women kind of sad. For one reason, I'm a couple of decades younger than him and if you took a picture of me on a corner in downtown Chicago, the only people you'd capture hanging on my arms would be panhandlers looking for spare change.

## PLAYBOY MEMORIES

I personally prefer to remember Hugh Hefner back in the 1960s, when he was the pipe smoking, pajama wearing, playboy of the Western World. I was about 13 when I first became aware of Playboy magazine. A bunch of my friends and I pooled our pocket change to buy our first copy of Playboy.

Although we were embarrassed to look at the magazine together, everyone wanted to have it first. So, through some perverse logic, the group decided to divvy up the contents of the magazine by cutting it into pieces. Because I was the youngest — or the only one of group who could read — I wound up with the sections on proper gentlemen's clothing, the Playboy Philosophy, and an interview with General Tito of Yugoslavia.

This ritual went on for years as I was growing up. I was 18 and I could still claim to be the only person in the country who actually did read Playboy for the articles. Go ahead, just ask me how to properly tie an ascot.

In the early 1960s, the Playboy empire was just getting rolling, opening Playboy Clubs all over the country. For $50 a year, a sophisticated and debonair gent could get a Playboy key. That key allowed entrance to Playboy Clubs anywhere in the world, where you could hobnob with celebrities like Peggy Cass and watch the Bunny waitresses do the "Bunny Dip" when they served your drinks.

So, my buddies and I got together, pooled our money and sent off for a Playboy Club key.

We were stunned when it arrived and we discovered there was no Playboy Club in our little town of 1,800 people. Nor was one ever likely to be built there, no matter how many letters we wrote to Hef and the magazine. They just kept sending us maps to the nearest clubs in Detroit, Lansing and Chicago.

## PLAYBOY CHICKEN CLUB

So, we opened our own Playboy Club. We painted an old door gold and put a Playboy Bunny symbol on it and hung it on a shed we found out in the woods. And we made everyone use the Playboy key to get in. Since we only had one key we had to hand it out the window every time someone showed up at the door so they could get in.

It wasn't exactly much of a bunny hutch. It was actually an old chicken coop — with chickens still in it. But that didn't stop us. We just decorated the shed with some "Bunny" pictures, put some candles on old crates covered with our mothers' hand-made doilies and pretended we were in a Playboy Club.

I have to say, though, the chickens made lousy "Bunny" hostesses. They were always getting feathers all over the place. And when we strapped those little bunny ears on them and put cotton balls on their chicken butts, they just looked plain ridiculous. Plus, they'd peck at you when you tried to order a drink.

Nevertheless, we'd go to our club once a day and sit around the wooden boxes and order dry martinis that tasted like Cherry Cola, and we'd discuss the Playboy Philosophy. Most people tend to think of Playboy as just being all nude pictures, but it actually provided a lot of advice to the young men of the era through the Philosophy and Playboy Adviser.

For example, we learned things like a gentleman always escorts his date by walking closest to the street himself, with his companion away for the curb. That supposedly would protect the lady from being splashed from the road. But, we all knew it meant that if a runaway car careened off the street unto the sidewalk, the guy would get killed first.

## WHAT'S A PLACKET?

Some of the stuff we read in the magazine made no sense to a bunch of teens sitting around a chicken shack in the woods. For example, the Playboy Adviser would tell us that our tie tack should always be affixed from the middle of the "shirt placket" so it centered on the front of your "Windsor knotted" tie.

"What do you think a placket is?" I would ask. "I don't know," my buddy, Charlie, would respond. "What's a tie tack? And who's Windsor?"

But we all diligently read the magazine's advice on how many blue, black and brown suits we should have in our wardrobe, even though we probably didn't have two suits between the six of us. And we became knowledgeable connoisseurs of cognac, fancy cars and stereo systems long before we reached the age or financial ability to buy any of those things.

Our makeshift hideaway lasted for a few years until we got to the dating age and could drive cars, and then we abandoned our Playboy Club and chose reality.

A few years ago, I went back to our old Playboy Club. The door was hanging off the shed. Its gold paint peeling, the old Bunny logo just faintly visible. It was a sad, sorry sight. But, my key still worked.

*My skiing technique in the early days consisted mainly of pointing my ski tips toward the bottom of the hill, saying a few silent prayers and pushing off.*

## SURVIVING DUMB KID TRICKS

This Sunday, as millions of Americans all over the world sit down to watch the XXIIIXXVXII Super Bowl on television, I will be out enjoying one of my favorite sports, downhill skiing.

While I love the sport, I am not very good at it. On occasions when I go, my family usually refer to my skiing excursion as "Dad's gone downhill screaming." They say this because of the cute way I like to call out to my fellow skiers as I pass them shouting, "Look out, look out, look ... oops sorry."

I got this reputation because early on when I first took up skiing, I couldn't seem to get the hang of how to turn, stop or do the snowplow, which is an excruciatingly painful maneuver that involves forcing your skis into a "V" shape with your legs while trying to avoid the tree in front of you.

I learned to ski in a place in southern Michigan called "Ski World," which was located in a big ravine unsuitable for farming. The owner, though, decided its steep, heavily wooded, rock covered cliffs would make it an incredibly dangerous place to ski. Locals called the place "Death World."

One of the unique features of Ski World was that all of its eight ski runs wound up in the same 10 square feet of land at the bottom of the ravine.

I'll tell you, there is nothing that gets the old blood racing and the adrenaline flowing through your veins faster than seeing 160 skiers coming down an icy hill with sharp pointy projectiles on their feet and hands heading for the exact same piece of land where you intend to crash.

My skiing technique in the early days consisted mainly of pointing my ski tips toward the bottom of the hill, saying a few silent prayers and pushing off. If nothing got in my way on the trip down, at the bottom of the ski run I would simply fall down or, if I was in an adventurous mood, I would sometimes ski out into the parking lot until I ran into a parked car.

## SKIING IN TRAFFIC

The first time I went to Ski World, I knew nothing about skiing and therefore had no knowledge of how dangerous this place was. In fact, my only previous skiing experience came from my childhood when one snowy winter day my brother, Stan, and I decided to take up skiing on the steep, busy street in front of our house.

Taking some old curtain rods from my mother's collection of old curtain rods under the basement steps, my brother and I nailed them to the bottom of some beat up shoes. Then we made poles by pounding some headless finishing nails into four fence slats that accidentally fell off the backyard fence. For protection, we would put on some old basketball knee pads and our football helmets and went out to ski down the steep sidewalk of our street.

Our first mistake was trying to walk up the hill with our makeshift skis. We looked like characters in an old silent film. For every step we made forward, we'd slide back five feet. When one of us got a foot or two up the hill, he would be grabbed by the other and dragged back. We were half way to the bottom of the hill before my brother discovered an old skiers trick for climbing a hill. We got down on all fours and scrambled up the hill on our hands and knees.

Now I've got to tell you, the hill we lived on was your typical old-fashioned city street. On the left side of the sidewalk were telephone poles, street signs and large solid trees one had to contend with. On the right side of the sidewalk were brick walls, wooden slat fences and hidden driveways to test your skills.

We stood at the top of the hill looking down this 3-foot-wide sidewalk with danger and death on either side and my brother says, "Looks like a pretty straight run to me. Want to race?"

Luckily, God, or good sense was with me that day, and I wisely declined his offer, suggesting instead he could go first since he was the oldest. "What's the matter? Are you chicken?" he asked.

Well, in those days, "chicken" was the worst thing you could call anyone. It could only be responded to by the come-back, "Oh, yeah. I'll show you who's chicken," which was then followed by some incredibly dangerous stunt like skiing down the sidewalk of a busy street with two curtain rods nailed to your feet and fence boards tied to your hands with nails sticking out.

## GOING FOR GOLD

So, I pointed my skis at the bottom of the hill, said a few silent prayers and pushed off. The first five or six seconds were pretty exciting. I went flashing down the hill, crouched over my curtain rods, wooden fencing tucked up under my arms like I'd seen skiers do. As I went zooming past our house, I caught the quickest glimpse of my mother in the front window with the most delighted and surprised look on her face. It looked almost like she was screaming, you know, cheering me on.

It was at that point I realized two things. One, I had no idea of how skiers stopped themselves from sliding very rapidly down a hill with curtain rods nailed to their shoes, and two, even if I did know how to stop, there was no place to do it unless I skied into a brick wall or went across the road and hit the steel mill fence at the bottom of the street.

Lucky for me, I had the traffic signal in my favor as I skied across the street and hit the fence. I'll tell you, if there had been an Olympic sport called sidewalk skiing and fence stop-ping, I would have scored a perfect "10" in competition and won a gold medal that day.

As I crawled back up the hill, wondering what had hap-pened to my brother, I found him a third of the way up hugging a tree and kissing it with his football helmet. We both survived somehow, basically unhurt, with the exception of the greeting we received from our mother when we got home.

"You two could have killed yourselves (*whack, whack*)." "Are you trying to scare me to death (*smack, smack*)?" "Now go put my curtain rods back under the steps (*pinch, pinch*)."

So you can see, after that experience, Ski World held no dangers in my mind. Actually, I picked up some very good skiing tips there. On my second trip down the hill, a ski instructor pulled me on the side and gave me some advice.

He said, "You have very nice form. I really like the way you crouch down and tuck those fence boards under your arms. But if you are ever going to be any good at this sport, I suggest you lose the curtain rods and get some real ski equipment."

# Chapter 7
# SURVIVING YOUR MOM

*Mom's are great. They birth us, raise us and give us words of advice like, "Don't chew your food with your finger up your nose." They also keep every bit of junk from our childhoods except things that have monetary value like baseball trading cards and old Barbie dolls. But we love them.*

*This new wave of "herbal healing" and holistic medication
to me is nothing more than the dreaded
"Mom's home remedies" in disguise.*

# SURVIVING HOME REMEDIES

I was out the other night with a friend, who pulled out a bunch of pill bottles that could have stocked a small pharmacy. He started taking them by the handful.

George explained his "Herbalist" had him taking zinc, ginseng, pectin, tree bark and several other natural medications recently discovered growing under a log in the rain forest to treat his sinus allergies.

"These natural medicines are going to unclog my liver, kidneys, lungs and pancreas," he said.

It seems his vital organs had become jammed with 20th century pollutants that were causing them to misfire and block up his nose.

As I listened to him expound on the benefits of herbal and natural treatments — "I can now breathe again from one nostril," he declared — I wondered why I hadn't yet jumped on the bandwagon of good health through seaweed extract.

Everywhere you look today, magical healing elixirs have become all the rage. No matter where you go, someone is touting the restorative properties of strange sounding compounds like Acidophilus and Omega 3 to Fatty Acid Fish Oil.

Almost daily I hear someone say, "I was having these migraine headaches, but then I started taking lecithin and titanium dioxide. Those two things combined with the frontal lobotomy have made me feel like a new man, yup, yup, wakadoo."

## FORGET GINKOBA

I have no way of telling whether these things work. For example, ginkoba is supposed to be good for your memory, but I keep forgetting to take it. And they say St. John's Wort will stop my snoring, but I'm usually asleep before it takes effect. I do know one thing. This new wave of "herbal healing" and holistic medication to me is nothing more than the dreaded "Mom's home remedies" in disguise.

When I was growing up, the medicine cabinet in my parents' home contained the usual necessities for curing most maladies. There was aspirin, Hydrogen Peroxide, bandages, Epsom Salt and a odorous green salve that looked and smelled like swamp moss. With those few supplies, my mother was able to handle any ailment or emergency from typhoid fever to the Black Plague.

Mom's theory of medicine was, anything that made you feel worse than you already did helped take your mind off of the real pain, which allowed the body to heal itself when no one was looking.

She'd pour stinging, burning Hydrogen Peroxide into open flesh wounds and go: "There, doesn't that feel better?"

Of course, I'd say, "Yes." Who wouldn't feel better having diluted battery acid poured onto their bleeding knee? I sure wasn't going to tell her it still hurt. She'd just pour more Hydrogen Peroxide on the wound.

But she just didn't stop with the Peroxide. Once the offending bruise had been sufficiently punished, she'd slap on a soothing coating of Tincture of Iodine, which came in a bottle with a skull and cross bones on it and a label that touted the medicine as "Poison." If that didn't make you just want to cry for joy, nothing did.

## NOT THE VAPORUB!

I don't want you to think my mother was mean. She just believed in these home cures that were probably developed to make heretics confess during the Spanish Inquisition. "Yes, indeed Inquisitor, draining all the blood from my body does make me feel better; please throw on a few more leeches."

One of the most feared weapons in Mom's arsenal of home healing products was the jar of Vicks Vaporub. With two aspirins and a glob of Vicks shoved up your nose, she could cure anything. Got a cold, pack your nose with Vicks. Laryngitis, cover your neck with Vicks. Skull fracture, fill the crack with Vicks.

It never took more than one dose of that mentholated, burning ointment and I was cured. Sometimes just the sight of the jar made all my symptoms go away.

"Honest Mom, the pain from the concussion disappeared all by itself. I won't need the Vicks."

If it was the flu season, Mom would boil up a kettle of water and put in two tablespoons of Vicks to sterilize the air in the house and possibly ward off evil spirits at the same time.

Vicks Vaporub was an all-around healer to my mom. She used it for arthritis, lumbago, muscle pain, athlete's foot—whatever needed fixing. I remember one time getting a painful muscle pull in my right leg. She rubbed it down with Vicks and put a heating pad on my leg. It took away the pain. In fact, it killed all the nerve endings in my upper thigh. I couldn't feel anything in my right leg for three years; except once in a while, it would mysteriously heat up without warning and make my eyes water.

The only medication in my mom's house that worked and didn't cause pain was the green swamp salve. It was made up every spring under a full moon, on the banks of the Monongahela River by an old man named Johnson who wore a chicken bone around his neck. This was powerful stuff. It could heal anything from snake bite to a broken rib. I once put it on a bad scalp rash and, not only did it clear up my dandruff, I grew six inches that summer.

I recently discovered an old can of the miracle green swamp salve in my mom's medicine cabinet with the label still attached. It's ingredients were listed on the can. I was shocked when I read them — "Two parts swamp moss, one part Vicks Vaporub." I threw the can away. I don't want holistic healers getting their hands on that secret.

*"They play music on Certificates of Deposits, now?" asked my mom. "When we had CDs, they just paid 7 percent interest. We didn't get any music with our CDs."*

# SURVIVING FAMILY DISCUSSIONS

My mother, who is 83, is visiting with us over the summer. My son Matt, 21, is also home right now. Counting my wife and I, we now have three generations living under one roof for a while. This has led to some very interesting intergenerational family discussions.

For example, Matt came home from work the other day and put on the stereo to blast out his favorite songs. I'm used to it, but the sudden wall of sound caused my mother to jump out of her chair, spin around three times, grab her heart and shout.

**Mom:** What's that noise? Is it an earthquake? Is the world ending?

**Matt:** (lowering the stereo) That's just the Dead Presidents.

**Mom:** The "deaf" presidents.

**Matt:** No, Grandma. It's the Dead Presidents.

**Mom:** Which ones?

**Me:** Probably Harding, Johnson and Millard Fillmore.

**Matt:** Who are they?

**Mom:** I think they were presidents. Matt, weren't you just talking about presidents?

**Matt:** Yes, the Dead Presidents. They're a music group.

**Mom:** Well, if that's music, they need more practice.

**Matt:** That's their sound, Grandma.

**Mom:** It sounds like noise to me. In my day, we had real songs like "In the Mood," and "Moonlight Serenade." And good musicians like Benny Goodman, Tommy Dorsey and Guy Lombardo. They made beautiful music. Why don't they make songs like that anymore?

**Matt:** I think it's because they died.

**Mom:** I mean the music. No one writes pretty songs anymore.

**Me:** It's probably because they wrote all the good songs back then and there's none left to do.

**Mom:** You mean all the good songs have been written?

**Me:** Right, the good stuff's all been written. So, the musicians had to move on and create new music like rock 'n' roll and disco.

**Mom:** Noise.

**Me:** Hey, I may agree with you about Matt's music, but now you're talking about my music. That was great stuff.

**Mom:** What great stuff? Elvis swiveling his hips (she does an imitation of Elvis swinging his hips) and singing "I ain't nothing but a hot dog."

**Me:** That's "Hound Dog."

**Matt:** And, besides, he's dead, too.

**Me:** We had some of the greatest musical groups of all times when I was growing up. We had the Beach Boys and the Beatles.

**Mom:** What did they sing that was so good?

**Me:** The Beach Boys sang "Little Deuce Coup" and "Good Vibrations." The Beatles did "I Wanna Hold Your Hand" and "Sgt. Pepper."

**Mom:** Noise.

**Matt:** Elevator music.

**Me:** Top 40 Golden Oldies.

**Matt:** TV commercial jingles.

**Me:** Classic Oldies.

**Mom:** More noise.

**Me:** Look, I'm going to get my 45s and show you both.

**Mom:** What's he getting?

**Matt:** A 45. It's a gun. Rock music has driven him crazy, Grandma. He's going to get a gun.

**Me:** No, Mom, They're records. Music used to come on 45 rpm records.

**Mom:** Ours came out of a Victrola.

**Matt:** What's a Victrola?

**Me:** It's a record player. You've seen the picture with the spotted dog listening to the machine with the cone on top. That's a Victrola.

**Matt:** So how did it play music?

**Me:** They used these big record disc called 78s that held the music.

**Matt:** Oh, like CDs.

**Mom:** They play music on Certificates of Deposits, now? When we had CDs, they just paid 7 percent interest. We didn't get any music with our CDs.

**Me:** A CD stands for compact disc. It's like a small record album that uses a laser to play the music.

**Mom:** Well, we didn't have no lasers in my day. They played music the old-fashioned way, with instruments. Like Glen Miller and his band. I used to love their song "Pennsylvania 6-5000."

**Matt:** Isn't that where the presidents live?

**Mom:** Which ones?

**Matt:** All of them.

**Me:** That's 1600 Pennsylvania Avenue.

**Mom:** No, I'm pretty sure it was "Pennsylvania 6-5000."

**Matt:** Wasn't there a movie by that name?

**Me:** That was "Transylvania 6-5000."

**Mom:** Isn't that where the White House is at?

**Matt:** No, it's in Washington, D.C.

**Mom:** I could have sworn it was "Pennsylvania 6-5000."

**Me:** That was a song.

**Mom:** I know it was a song.

**Matt:** How'd it go?

**Mom:** It went (singing), "Pennsylvania 6-5000."

**Matt:** And....?

**Me:** That was it. They just sang a phone number—the whole song. And she thinks Elvis lyrics are bad.

**Mom:** It was enough.

**Matt:** Who's phone number was it anyway?

**Mom:** Probably the president's phone number. He lives on Pennsylvania Avenue.

**Matt:** Which president?

**Mom:** One of the dead ones.

*Going to the house I grew up in is like walking into a museum dedicated to the 1950s. Everything still looks the same as when Eisenhower was president.*

# SURVIVING THE NOSTALGIA HIGHWAY

I took a drive on the nostalgia highway this week and went back to my home in Ohio. I don't know about you, but the place where I grew up will always be home to me no matter where I live or how far I move away from it.

Going home always makes me feel younger. It's like time travel. When I pull out of the driveway of my house, I'm an aging Baby Boomer with worries about work, bills, mortgages and whether I've packed enough dental floss for the trip. But as each mile of the trip rolls on, the clock ticks backward through the stages of my life until I finally show up on the doorstep of our house as a 12-year-old, calling out, "Mom, I'm home."

And she answers back in our ritualistic exchange, "Well, wipe your feet. I just vacuumed the floor.''

Going to the house I grew up in is like walking into a museum dedicated to the 1950s. Everything still looks the same as when Eisenhower was president and I used to watch "Howdy Doody"        lying on the living room floor. They could probably reshoot scenes from "Leave it to Beaver" in my mother's house and not have to change so much as the white plastic clock on the kitchen wall with the hour and minute hands that still glow in the dark at night from the radioactive paint on them that was banned from use in 1961.

Like the house, the clock stopped moving into the future sometime in the late 1950s. But it still sits on the wall watching over my mom as it has these past 45 years or more.

"Mom, why don't you let me get rid of that old clock and buy you a new one," I say every time I go home, even though I know the answer by heart. "Let it go. I've got other clocks to use," she says, pointing to the sundial on the 1952 Amana gas range that sits in the kitchen like a small white Volkswagen Beetle.

## OUTLIVING APPLIANCES

At age 83, my mother's fondest wish is to die before all of her appliances break and she has to buy new ones. The toll on the aging household fixtures, once held at bay by my father's fix-it abilities, has accelerated in the years since he passed away. The picture tube in the old Phillips TV console bought back in 1957 went out last winter. So, it sits in the living room, displaying old knickknacks and yesterday's advertising fliers. A vintage portable radio, big as a suitcase, sits beside my father's recliner, still set to a channel that now only plays static.

"They just don't make these things to last anymore," Mom says, rummaging through an old Frigidaire refrigerator — one of two in the house — that no longer works except as a cupboard for canned goods.

As I feel my way through the rooms, lighted by 40 watt bulbs my mother insists are "good enough to see by," I come across photos of my brother and me hung on the living room walls. The photo gallery chronicles our advancement from toddlers through high school graduation. I looked pretty dapper in that photo with my Bryl-creamed pompadour and shiney one-inch-wide tie.

On an end table, I spy an ugly ceramic ashtray with a red-nosed reindeer I made in Junior Achievement in the 10th grade. The red nose was my trademark. I told everyone they'd be collector's items someday, and I was right. My mother's got a dozen of them collecting dust in the attic.

She keeps urging me to take some back to Michigan to give away as gifts for my friends. I tell her no one I know smokes anymore, but if they start up again, I'll take them an ashtray.

# THE BEDROOM MUSEUM

Up in my bedroom, things are pretty well as I left them 30 years ago when I went off to college. Not a stick of furniture has been moved. The same green-and-white tufted bed cover my grandmother made lays atop the concrete hard mattress bought to protect my young spine from curvature.

A nautical lamp above my bed tilts jauntily to the side. Right next to it is a pennant from my high school days. I go to my desk in front of the window and open a drawer. Inside is decades-old homework, still unfinished. I close the drawer quickly, knowing some things are best left untouched.

In another drawer, I find collectors' copies of old "Popular Mechanics" magazines, with pictures of backyard barbecue grills and cement patios still being built on the covers.

Moving to the closet, I rummage through boxes of old Valentines and Mother's Day cards my mom has kept from me and my brother. In another box, I find crayon-colored pictures of little angels and birdies embossed with my name. Still clinging to them like they were glued on yesterday are the gold and silver stars I earned in second-grade reading class.

Old shoe boxes that once held Keds and Florsheim footwear now store the memories of my childhood like cardboard time capsules to be opened only on visits home.

Finally, it's night, and tired from my day traveling the nostalgia highway, I fall asleep under the quilt my grandmother made me, surrounded by history, in the home my parents built for us on Memory Lane.

*I once went out to get some milk and bread for the kids
and saw a "for sale" sign on the way to the store
and came home with a 1988 Buick.*

## SURVIVING THE SALE GENE

I have discovered that my family has a hereditary ailment that forces us to buy things whether we need the stuff or not, as long as it's on sale. From what I've come to understand, this illness has been passed on in my family for centuries through the "shopping gene."

The shopping gene — and there is one because I've seen it under a microscope I bought on sale at the Healthcare R Us store — is shaped like a small rectangular sign with the words "Must buy something" stenciled in the middle.

The gene, which was isolated and identified by researcher Wally Mart, causes family members to lose all control when confronted by a sale sign. It doesn't make any difference if it appears at the grocery store, clothing shop, garage sale or car dealership. When we see a sale sign, our eyes glaze over, our heart rates go up and, without thinking, we are overcome by an overwhelming urge to pick something up and buy it.

You might find this funny, but I once went out to get some milk and bread for the kids and saw a "for sale" sign on the way to the store and came home with a 1988 Buick.

"Where's the milk and bread?" my wife asked when I returned to the house. "Oh, it's in the back seat of the Buick I just bought," I said, trying to subtly break the news to her.

As near as I can tell, all members of my mother's side of the family are affected by the gene. My Aunt Stella is a prime example. Whenever we stop by to see her, we call it "visiting Stella's store." My aunt has acquired more canned goods, bottled salad dressing, skillet dinners, soda pop and snacks than is carried by the average supermarket. A visit to her place is usually called "rotating the stock" because no one leaves her house without a bag of groceries under each arm.

You don't even have to be a member of the family to get groceries from Aunt Stella. I was there one day when a Girl Scout showed up selling cookies. My aunt bought some cookies after talking the girl into a discount, then sent the girl away with a jumbo-sized box of laundry detergent and some fabric softener.

## GETTING THE GOODS

My aunt says she doesn't know why she buys all these things, most of which she doesn't need or use. "It's just the challenge of the hunt that's exciting," she says, recently having bagged $25 worth of groceries for $3.29 using her collection of "$1.00 off coupons" on "double coupon" day, along with a 10 percent discount from her AARP card.

She is not the only one in our family who does this stuff. My brother, Stan, years ago, converted his two-car garage into a food storage warehouse for stocking sale items and bulk food buys. The place is stacked from floor to ceiling with shelves filled with enough food to keep a busy restaurant going for several years. It is rumored that when the national discount retailer, "Sam's Club," decided to go into business, it based its store design on my brother's garage.

I'm no different than them. I go out several times a week early in the morning, hunting down discounted sale items at the local supermarket. The other day, I was at Frank & Bubba's Shoppe and Bag and I came across a sale on elk-flavored spaghetti sauce for 29 cents a gallon. I bought ten.

Then I bought five pounds of Squid Linguine for a dollar. I also bought some kitty litter, a dozen cans of Frisky Gourmet and some catnip I found in the discount bin. We don't presently own a cat, but you never know when one might go on sale.

The flip side of the buying gene my family shares is that, after a certain age, it starts to wear out. Instead of buying stuff in mass quantities, we start giving stuff away. My Aunt Stella is obviously in the transitional stage.

My mom after decades of shrewd buying has turned the corner and is now giving everything away. I go visit my mom and she goes, "Why don't you take that sofa home with you, I don't need it anymore. And take this chair with you. I sit too much anyway."

I can see signs that I'm nearing this stage, too. In fact, if anyone wants any elk-flavored spaghetti sauce for free, just give me a call.

*Why my mother would keep 3,000 plastic container lids is a wonder to me. What was even stranger was why she only had 1,000 containers.*

## SURVIVING MOM'S MOVE

Attention! This is a special announcement for anyone who is over 50 years of age. Please go home immediately and begin cleaning the clutter out of your house.

Drop whatever you are doing and go to your local grocery store and get 40 large garbage bags and several dozen cardboard boxes and begin tossing out every receipt and scrap of paper dated before the original George Bush was president.

Box up the souvenirs from your trip to Atlantic City 20 years ago, including the unopened but possibly still edible Salt Water Taffy, and throw it out. Toss in the white "Go, Go" boots from the 1960s, the David Cassidy fan club desk blotter, all your old eight-track tapes of Captain and Tenille and the broken "Pong" game hidden in the back of the closet. Then dump it all.

Do that and your children will be forever in your debt.

The reason I know that is because I just got back from spending a week at my mother's house, clearing out similar items.

After living in the same house for 52 years, my mom decided the place was too much to take care of and moved into a nursing center. She moved in with two suitcases of clothes and a handful of pictures. And she is happy. Of course Mom is happy, she didn't have to deal with getting rid of 3,000 plastic container lids like I did.

Why my mother would keep 3,000 plastic container lids is a wonder to me. What was even stranger was why she only had 1,000 containers.

I asked her why there were more lids than containers and Mom confided to me very seriously, "Lids are much harder to come by."

# MOM SAVED EVERYTHING

As any good mother worth her salt, my mother saved everything. Going through filing cabinets and desk drawers I turned up every report card my brother and I ever produced, all the merit badges I earned as a Boy Scout, canceled checks dating back to 1952, dog tags from a long-buried pet, water, electric and gas bills for the past five decades, and a dozen books of Green Stamps.

What I wanted to know was where was the old shoe box of baseball trading cards that my brother and I had with the rookie year cards from Roger Marris and Mickey Mantel. It also contained a bunch of valuable collector cards of Ty Cobb and Babe Ruth, if memory serves me right. That stuff I couldn't find.

"Where did the baseball cards go?" I asked my mother.

"Oh, I threw that stuff out. It was cluttering up the house," she said.

For those of you who are of a mind to save things to pass on to your children and grandchildren, here are a few rules I have developed that are based on common sense. Please cut these out and tape them to your refrigerator, or at the very least, have them tattooed on your arm.

## TEN THINGS NOT TO SAVE FOR YOUR KIDS

1. Shoes, especially old shoes
2. Used aluminum foil
3. Empty medicine bottles with cotton in them
4. McDonald's sugar, salt and pepper packs
5. Dented Styrofoam cups
6. Ten years worth of newspaper fliers
7. Books by Mickey Spillane
8. Letters from the Postmaster General announcing rate increases
9. Petrified bread ends in plastic bags
10. Plastic container lids

## FINDING THE TREASURES

She also saved treasures of the heart too valuable to surrender. There were my father's golfing trophies, earned in a career of amateur golf played through the summers and falls of his life. In my bedroom, under my high school diploma, I found a collection of paint-by-numbers paintings that I remember creating with my family while sitting around the kitchen table on Saturday nights.

In the big chest of drawers in the living room were hundreds of pictures of family members and friends long gone, but still alive and smiling out at me through the years in the black-and-white Kodak prints. Alongside them I find bundles of letters and Christmas cards, and Mother's Day and Father's Day cards my brother and I sent over the years, tied with care in red ribbon.

I pack these things away carefully in boxes and bring them home with me to be stored with love in the back of my closet. Someday, hopefully, my children can find them among my plastic lid collection, old shoes and Mickey Spillane books, and they, too, will wonder why I ever saved this stuff.

*I know a lot of things have changed today in this fast-paced, super-hyper world we live in, but I believe mothers today still find time to be moms.*

# SURVIVING WORDS OF WISDOM

It's Mother's Day this Sunday, and I'd like to send a tribute out to my mom and every other mother out there who has made the loving sacrifice to go through nine months of morning sickness, back pains, hormonal changes, swollen feet, maternity clothes and hours of labor to produce a new human being.

To a child, a mom is there to nurture you, comfort you when you are sick or hurt, and raise you from a helpless infant to the point where the child says, "Look Mom, I'm my own person now. I don't need your help anymore, but stay close to the phone in case it doesn't work."

Whether she's called "Mommy," "Mama," "Mom, "Mum," or a hundred derivatives of the name "Mother," a mom will do a thousand things for you, from making your world a safe place to sacrificing her dreams so you can have dreams of your own. She is the one who finds your lost toys when you cry and sews on your buttons when you lose one, but only after she has carefully searched your crib, playpen, the house and your diaper to find the lost button and make sure you didn't swallow it.

I know a lot of things have changed today in this fast-paced, super-hyper world we live in, but I believe mothers today still find time to be moms. They are still the ones who help you learn the tools of life from an early age. They teach you how to count your little piggies, play peak-a-boo, wave bye-bye, use the pottie, and they still feed you strained carrots without letting you get too much in your hair and on your clothes.

My mom was big on baby things. She loves to tell the story of how when I was a baby I used to take the bowl when I was done eating and rub it on my head to get extra nutrients. "It was cute," she says. Luckily for me, she doesn't come to where I work to tell that story anymore.

150

# WORDS TO LIVE BY

As I grew up, Mom was always there to provide me with words of wisdom, counsel and advice on life. After talking to other people, I find that they weren't original thoughts, but may in fact be special messages that have been passed down from mother to child since the beginning of time.

My mom would say:

*"Eat your carrots. They're good for your eyes. You never see rabbits wearing glasses."*

*"Don't run with scissors in your hand. You'll poke your eye out."*

*"Close the door. You weren't raised in a barn."*

*"Don't speak with your mouth full. It's not polite."*

*"Wear clean underwear. You never know when you might be in an accident."*

That was my mother's credo and you know what? I ate my carrots, walked with the scissor blades clutched tightly in my hand, shut all doors on entering and ate with my mouth closed for decades. And the one time I was in a car accident and had to go to the emergency room, I had clean underwear on. Aren't you proud of me, Mom?

My mother's wisdom saved me on many occasion while I was growing up. On the other hand, my father was the easiest touch in the world. All I had to do to get his approval was tell him that my mother had said 'yes' to whatever I wanted to do, and he'd agree.

I'd ask him if I could go play in the old stone quarry and swim in the bottomless lake that was there, and he'd ask, "What did your mother say?" And I'd answer, "She said it was OK as long as I didn't go anywhere near the quarry and I stayed out of the water." My father would nod his head in thoughtful agreement and say, "Then it's fine with me, too." I used to get my father in so much trouble.

With my mother, it was always much more difficult. If I told her everyone in the neighborhood was going to the quarry, she'd say, "Well, if everyone jumped off a cliff, would you do it too?" I'd say "yes" because that's exactly what we did when we went to the quarry.

Unfortunately, or fortunately as case may be, she wouldn't let me go and I would cry, "But Mom, everyone's going. Why can't I go?" And in her infinite wisdom, she would answer, "Because I said so, that's why."

Well, thankfully, my quarry swimming days are over. I've survived my childhood and adolescent traumas and grown into a mature adult who has a family and my own kids, and there's only one thing I want to say to my mother: "Thank you for being there and I love you."

# Chapter 8
# SURVIVING KIDS

*Kids come into your life and take it over. You give them your love, time and energy and then they grow up and go off to start their own lives. How rude. But whether they get married, go to the military, off to college, or move into a box in your basement. You'll miss them.*

*It's really hard to believe 25 years has passed since our
first child was born. The time has gone faster than
I ever expected, or dreamed possible.*

# SURVIVING KIDS LEAVING HOME

Our son Jason is graduating next week. Every day he puts
on his cap and gown and practices looking cool in front of the
mirror. It's a monumental day for him, and his parents, who very
soon will be finding out what the term "empty nesters" means.

Like his two brothers before him, Jason will be leaving
the shelter of his loving home, abandoning his mom and dad who
loved and raised him and still have his first pair of booties packed
away somewhere, to move out into the cold hard world.

I can remember back when I was graduating from high
school, though, and feeling the exact same way. But now, as a
parent watching the last of our three sons prepare to leave home,
I don't think it's such a good idea.

It's really hard to believe 25 years have passed since our
first child was born. The time has gone faster than I ever expected or dreamed possible.

Nathan, the artist who wore two different color tennis
shoes all through high school as a statement against the
administration's restrictive dress code (shoe color wasn't covered), becomes a teacher this fall, shaping young minds and tal-
ents. Matthew, the trained Ninja who played GI Joe with his
friends in our backyard, is preparing for Army Air Assault camp
and completion of his Officers' Training School with hopes of
becoming a combat helicopter pilot, in wars that we hope will
never come.

And Jason, our special son and promising Elvis imper-
sonator, is out looking for traditional employment while waiting
for his big break in Las Vegas or with the FBI, whichever comes
along first.

# WHERE DID THE TIME GO?

It seems like just last week they were borrowing money against their allowances to buy the original Star War figures, and now they're using those same toys to finance down payments on cars. (Aren't you guys glad I didn't throw them out?) An instant ago, I was teaching them how to tie their shoes and button their shirts, and now they can dress themselves. Yesterday, I taught them how to play baseball and tomorrow they'll be teaching their own kids the game.

One day they're little kids dependent on you for everything and the next they're adults ready to define the future of a next millennium. I don't know if I'm comfortable with that thought. It's not that I don't trust them. Heck, I gave them to the keys to the 1967 Mustang ever since they started to drive and never cringed once when doing it. It's the short drive from parent and protector to "onlooker" in their lives that bothers me.

No longer will I be able to say "don't climb that tree." From now on I'll be saying things like "I really think mutual funds are a better long term investment that a jet ski."

I also keep wondering what we're going to do with all those empty bedrooms. Do we turn them into game rooms? There'll be no one around any more to play games with except Madeline, my spouse, and she's not much of a game player except for checkers and you don't need three whole rooms for playing checkers. I guess we could rent their rooms out, but we didn't build those bedrooms for strangers. Besides where would we store the boys' stuff until the next time they come home?

Right now, they're all home for the summer. Nate and Matt have brought home a truck load of laundry that stretches from the washer across the laundry room, down the hall and into the family room. The garage is full of things they might be taking with them in the fall, the storage room in the basement is a staging area for things they may or may not need, but which they want to hang on to for a while longer. And their bedrooms are filled wall-to-wall with the important stuff of their daily lives since preschool — those personal possessions and favorite mementos they want to keep forever.

I look over these things they brought home with them from school. There's the lifelike plastic severed hand, a talking "Tick" doll, a half-eaten box of Slim Jims, several Luke Skywalker Light Sabers, a pith helmet and a copy of the "Joke Teller's Handbook." What have these kids been studying in college? Intermixed with these things are 365 pairs of rolled socks, some broken radios, 14 stereo speakers, a tiger print lamp shade, several dismantled loft beds, something called a futon, miles of extension cords, and a dozen rolls of toilet paper (at last something we can use around the house).

It's all here for "temporary" storage until they get where they're going. Which probably means we'll store it here forever, like our parents did with our stuff. The way I look at it is the kids may leave you, but their things never move out of your home.

*Whether your son or daughter has gone off to college, the military, gotten married or moved into a closet in the basement and now takes their meals through a slot in the door, you'll miss them.*

# SURVIVING THE EMPTY NEST

Our friends, Lester and Marilyn, sent out an e-mail message the other day to announce that their three children where finally all off to school, on their own and officially out of the house. Along with the announcement they also had this question, "Now that they're gone, what do we do beside worry?"

Having gone through this empty nest experience, I gave them this advice.

What you do now is wait. You wait for their phone calls. You wait for them to come home on vacations and holidays. You wait for college bills that keep pouring in like water from a broken faucet that won't shut off for the next four, five or six years.

The phone calls usually come collect — and late at night. The calls go something like this. "Hi, Mom and Dad. Guess who this is calling you at 3 a.m. just to say hi."

As you sit on the edge of the bed waiting for your heart to stop pounding because you know any phone call that comes in after midnight is bad news, they tell you about all of the exciting things that have been going on at school. You'll be happy for them. They're young. They're having fun. Life is exciting for them. You should encourage them. I like to call them back the next morning at 6 a.m., get them out of bed, and tell them how happy I am for them.

## VACATION TIME

You'll also get used to waiting for their school vacations to roll around. Vacations are when your kids come home to spend time with you, their loving family. They'll be home, unless they get a better offer to go skiing in the Rockies or visit someone else's parents' home in Miami Beach.

Visits home are usually marked by four things. Your children will be thrilled at seeing you, getting their laundry done, sleeping and tracking down old friends to go out with them.

And, of course, visits home from college usually mean your child is separated from their newly found love interest, who they will have to call seven-to-eight times a day while they're apart. By the time vacation is over, you will have seen your kids a total of 20 minutes in seven days and you wonder where the time has flown.

## SILENCE OF THE PHONES

Whether your son or daughter has gone off to college, the military, gotten married or moved into a closet in the basement and now takes their meals through a slot in the door, you'll miss them.

Your house will be quieter. There will be no stereos blaring, no Nintendo bombs exploding, no doors slamming and no phones ringing. People with strange names like "Dweezle," "Ratface" and "Mongo" will stop calling your house at all hours of the day. And that's just the girls.

I think the silence of the phone was the most unnerving change when our youngest son, Matt, went off to school. When he was home, the phone would start ringing at 7 a.m. and wouldn't stop until midnight. I'd come home after work and there would be 36 phone messages for him on the answering machine and one for me from the video store announcing that 14 videos rented in my name last weekend were now seven days overdue.

Then Matt was off to school and the phone stopped ringing. I thought it was broken. I called the phone company six times that week to see if we were still connected. I'd go, "Is my phone still working? We haven't heard from Dweezle in days."

## YOUR LIFE HAS CHANGED

There's no denying it. Once your children go off on their own, your life is different. For one thing, the refrigerator door will stay closed for long periods of time. And the kitchen will stay clean, also for long periods of time. You'll also notice that long-standing food essentials like Nutty Bars, HoHos, Ding Dongs, potato chips, Doritos, salsa, peanut butter, yogurt, breakfast bars, Twizzlers and Starbursts — the basics of most teen diets — will sit uneaten in the pantry and eventually disappear from the shopping list.

The lights in your house will stay shut off when you turn them off. The gas gauge on your car won't dive to empty every time you start it. The television will stay tuned to the PBS station instead of automatically putting on "Nick at Nite." Grass in your yard will stay unmowed unless you mow it.

There are other things you'll notice, too.

Pictures of your kids will become more meaningful to you. Letters and e-mails from them will become treasures you carry around with you and reread during the day. Boxes of their childhood school work and drawings you've been meaning to throw out will suddenly become precious mementos to you. And their bedrooms, which you had secretly thought of turning into an office, study or guest room someday, will remain just the way they left them for when they come home again.

They may be grown and gone, but they'll always be in your heart.

*"Why would anyone put the mail in the dryer?" I cried. My kids looked at me like I was out of my head. "Dad, we had to dry it after it went through the washer."*

## SURVIVING COLLEGE KIDS

Please help me. I've been cut off from all communication with the outside world for the past six weeks. No, it wasn't a natural disaster like a flood or hurricane that caused this disruption. And it wasn't a tornado knocking out our electricity and phone lines. It's worse. The kids have come home from college for the summer and they've taken control of the phones, mail, television and radios in our house.

It wasn't too long ago I would get 12 to 15 phone calls a day. Now, I'm down to getting roughly — none. The reason is the boys these days are either on the phone, answering the phone or taking my messages off the answering machine and hiding them in strange places.

They work in shifts at this, with my son Jason handling the morning phone work while his brother Nathan relieves him after lunch. After 4 p.m., the three of them play tag-team phone calling during the evening hours. Here's the way it works. The telephone rings and one them yells, "It's for me" grabs the portable and that's the last we see of the phone for the week.

We have "call waiting" on our phone. That's a second incoming call line on which people can get through if someone's on the phone. But, the boys use it to talk to two people at once. So, not only can't we use the phone, no one else can get through to us, either.

Even when they go out, we still can't get calls. My one son hooked up a  new super computer answering machine in his bedroom to our phone line and now it overrides my answering machine, intercepting the calls and telling people they've reached, "Charlie's House of Pancakes."  I was away on vacation when the machine started doing this and I had to rush home to find out why this guy "Charlie" had opened a pancake house in my kitchen.

# ED MCMAHON CALLING

I finally took a stance and demanded everyone start writing down phone messages for their mother and me. I did it after we got a letter from Ed McMahon saying we had won the $1,000,000 Publisher's Clearinghouse Sweepstakes but since they couldn't reach us because our phone was always busy, and the few messages Ed left on "Charlie's House of Pancakes" machine never got returned, they gave the money to some single guy with no kids who answers his own phone.

While I've gotten the kids to be more responsible about this, we're still out of the touch with the world. For some reason, the boys seem unable to grasp the concept that messages—to get delivered—have to be:

1) written down, preferably on paper with a writing instrument like a pen or pencil;
2) contain the caller's name, phone number and message;
3) be left in an obvious place where they might be found eventually.

As an example, late this summer I realized I hadn't heard anything on my appointment to the Senate Subcommittee on Nuclear Disarmament and asked my son, Matt, if I'd gotten any calls. He said, "Somebody called you about something and you're supposed to call them back." I asked when they had called. "June," he said. "And they said it was urgent."

He said he'd written the message down on the old tin pie pan we keep under the sink to catch drips. "So where is it?" I asked, not finding the pan under the sink where it's supposed to be. Matt said, "It's outside on the patio with water in it for the dog."

So, I went out and after fighting off the dog who was trying to get a drink, I looked in the pan and written on the bottom under the water was the message "Dad, somebody called about something. Call them at 202-64..." The rest of the number had been lapped away by the dog and, along with it, any hope of world peace.

## LAUNDERING THE MAIL

I have to say the other two boys are much more responsible about taking phone messages. They take down the complete message, name and phone number and then put it with the mail. The only problem is, no one puts the mail where it might reasonably be discovered. One day, they put it on top of the refrigerator. The next day, it's in the refrigerator. Last week, I found a stack of mail and messages in the clothes dryer.

"Why would anyone put the mail in the dryer?" I cried. My kids looked at me like I was out of my head. "Dad, we had to dry it after it went through the washer," said the oldest with obvious logic. Despite the inconvenience, I did have to admit that the mail was nice and warm and fluffy and had never smelled fresher, even if there was no legible writing left on it.

If you're wondering why I don't just use a cellular phone, it's because a week after the boys got home, it disappeared, although I can still hear it ringing somewhere in the house, late at night when I'm going to sleep.

I think the worst part of losing communication with the outside world is not knowing what's going on out there. The kids not only have taken over the phone but also the television channel changer, and they've somehow programmed out everything with news content, so now we only get Comedy Central, QVC buying channel and reruns of the "Brady Bunch."

The only way I knew the Chicago Bulls won the NBA championship and the Red Wings the Stanley Cup was because they were selling team championship sweatshirts on QVC. I have no perspective anymore on world events, but I do know Marcia Brady has a new boyfriend and I know what happened to Cartman's father.

This problem has reached the point where I've had to take drastic measures. So, as of today, I'm moving out of the house to a phone booth  on the beach, where I've forwarded my mail and put in cable. It's not much of a place, but the view is beautiful.

*As father of the groom, my responsibility so far has been to get myself fitted for a tuxedo. I also get to say "Hmmm" a lot.*

# SURVIVING YOUR CHILD'S WEDDING

In just about three weeks, our son Nathan will be getting married. Our baby boy is all grown up now and ready to embark on the next stage of life's continual voyage.

It's hard to believe that just 10 months ago we got the call announcing the engagement. It came at 3 a.m.

My wife, Madeline, as is her habit with 3 a.m. phone calls, jumped up and grabbed the ringing phone, demanding, "Who got hurt? Where was the accident?"

Then all of a sudden, she was crying and going "Oh, that's wonderful. Congratulations," while I lay there in my sleep-deprived state, wondering what kind of accident could be so wonderful that people congratulated you on it.

But when I heard her go, "So when are you thinking of setting the wedding date?" I knew our son had proposed to his girlfriend, Kyla King.

He had proposed to Kyla on the sixth anniversary of the first time they met, which was at a Halloween party at Michigan State University. The old romantic had decided that proposing at a Halloween party at MSU would be an appropriate time to pop the big question.

We had seen them just before the party. Our son, an art teacher, was dressed as Impressionist painter Vincent Van Gogh, complete with missing ear. Kyla, a newspaper reporter for The Grand Rapids Press, was dressed as a clown. As I ran the visualization of this through my head, I realized our son had just gotten engaged to .... oh, no.... a reporter.

## WEDDING PLANS

They set the wedding date for Aug. 5 of this year and, if memory serves me correctly, by the day after the engagement all of the wedding arrangements and invitations had been made and sent. Ushers and bridesmaids selected. Hall rented and the wedding banquet planned. I'm sure it didn't happen that quick, but it seems that way.

As father of the groom, my responsibility so far has been to get myself fitted for a tuxedo.

I also get to say "Hmmm" a lot. I found early on that's the best way to handle being shown any pictures of floor-length dresses, bridal gowns, wedding cakes, engraved invitations or satin pillows the ring bearers will carry.

Here's how it works:

Madeline: "What do you think of my wearing this dress for the wedding?"

Me: "Hmmm."

Madeline: "You're right I don't think it's my color. How about this one?"

Me: "Hmmm."

Madeline: "I like it too. I'll keep this one in mind."

So far, my wife has bought three dresses to wear to the wedding plus a completely different set of foundation garments and shoes for each outfit. Myself, I bought new underwear and socks. Hmmm.

Another word the father of the groom and the father of the bride use a lot is the word "Wow." As in "Wow, that's a beautiful wedding dress."

The word "Wow" is also used a lot as an exclamation before the words "I didn't realize." Here's an example:

"Wow, I didn't realize _____ (fill in the blank with "flowers," "wedding cakes," "invitations," "photographs," "hors d'oeuvres," "punch" or "weddings") cost so much."

In preparation for the wedding, my wife, Madeline, and I have been going through the family photo albums, collecting pictures of Nathan growing up which will go along side the King family photos of Kyla growing up, so both families can embarrass their children on their wedding day.

# PICTURES FROM THE PAST

In the batch we've selected, we have one of Nathan as a little baby, raising his head from the blanket and looking around to see where the action is. There's another of his first haircut, with Mom collecting the snips of soft blond hair in an envelope for posterity.

I found one of Nathan taking his first wobbly bike ride and going off the path and hitting a tree. And next is the picture of him with his arm in a sling after the ride.

Also in the pile of childhood memories will be the picture of the young, future artist winning a ribbon at the county fair for his hand-painted ceramic raccoon. It still sits in his room on the dresser next to baseball and acting awards he won from grade school on up.

Then there's Nate's "Miami Vice" year, and a picture of him looking like Don Johnson in a pale blue suit and T-shirt. We still have that suit somewhere, probably saving it for his kids.

There are pictures scattered throughout of him and his brothers, Jason and Matt, growing up together, making mischief, having fun as brothers do.

High school photos are full of Nathan and his young friends, hanging all over each other and generally goofing around. There are photos of Nathan at the prom all dressed up in his tuxedo, another in casual school clothes with two different colored tennis shoes (it's a long story), and one with Nate in his football uniform. He was a tenacious tackle and made "all city" that year on a football team that won only one game.

At college, he chose art over football, turning everyday objects like boxes of Kraft Macaroni and Cheese into art. There are pictures of him and new friends at college — the "Cedar Street" boys and girls.

As I thumb through the pictures of his life at Michigan State, one particularly lovely young girl keeps appearing in more and more photos. It's Kyla. One of the last photos in the book is a picture of Van Gogh holding hands with a clown. It's their engagement picture. I think we'll make that one the centerpiece of our photo memories.

*Somehow during the last decade we adopted the rule that
anything that comes into our house can never leave.
Our home has become the "Hotel California"
for possessions.*

# SURVIVING GARAGE SALE MEMORIES

Last Saturday, I attempted that unique American house-cleaning ritual known as the garage sale. This was to be the first garage sale I'd hosted in about seven years and I looked forward with anticipation to unloading all of the stuff I had gathered together in my garage for this day.

As I sat in the warm September sun, my price sheet neatly typed on the card table beside me and my pockets full of change, I thought back on how much this ritual had changed for my wife, Madeline, and I over the years.

When we were first married, back in the days before Disco shoes where invented, we were so poor we couldn't even think of holding a garage sale because everything we owned was needed. The first time we moved from one small apartment to a slightly bigger small apartment, we put everything we owned in a 6-foot by 6-foot U-Haul trailer and still had room inside for break dancing. The last time we moved, it took a semi-truck and a half dozen car trips to get all of our stuff relocated.

Somehow during the last decade we adopted the rule that anything that comes into our house can never leave. Our home has become the "Hotel California" for possessions.

It wasn't always that way. When we bought our first house we discovered the necessity of garage sales as a hidden source of income to be dipped into whenever we needed extra cash. The muffler on the car would break, we'd hold a garage sale. Income taxes due, we'd hold a garage sale. Want to go out for dinner on our anniversary, hold a garage sale. Sometimes we held six or seven a month. I'd go, "There's a good movie at the drive-in tonight, want to have a garage sale and go?"

## OUTGROWN ON WEDNESDAY

That all changed as the economy improved in the 1980s and our three boys began to outgrow their clothes faster than we could wash and fold them. That's no joke. It was like buy the boys pants at Sears on Monday, they'd wear them on Tuesday, outgrow them on Wednesday, and Thursday we'd wash and put them away for the next garage sale.

Plus, we had all these old matchbox cars and Star Wars toys they didn't play with anymore that we had to get rid of to make room for more things they'd outgrow. (By the way, if anyone still has any of the Star Wars figures I sold for 25 cents apiece, I'd like them back now. Thank you.)

So once a summer, we'd bring out these boxes and boxes of kids clothes and worthless junk that we'd sell in mammoth garage sales. We did it not to make money, but to unload the house to make room for future garage sale things.

My philosophy for garage sales in those days was get rid of everything, quickly. The more they bought, the cheaper it got. Buy two undersized boys sweatshirts for a buck, get a only-used-once, size 6, $40 Easter suit free. Purchase a half dozen INXS T-shirts for 50 cents, I'd throw in the old 19-inch broken color TV for nothing.

Our house in those days was just a temporary home for goods destined to other homes. Unfortunately, the more things I sold, the more things we acquired. I once completely cleaned out everything in our home, sold the house and moved to a different town. When I got up in the morning in our new place, I couldn't find the living room because of the stuff that had appeared there overnight. We had to hold another garage sale just so we could find the kids.

## GARAGE SALE HEIRLOOMS

But last week, the garage sale was different. This time, I wasn't selling off junk that would someday be collectors' items, and I wasn't disposing of old outgrown clothes to make room for new outgrown clothes. This time—with the boys out of the house and on their own—I was, it seems, selling off priceless, irreplaceable family heirlooms and mementos.

"You're selling our children's memories," Madeline cried, clutching to her bosom a size 3, moth-eaten basketball shirt with our son Matt's name on it. "How can you do this?"

Madeline picked up a lamp shade made out of four different kinds of pasta and held it to her cheek. "Jason gave this to me for Mother's Day in 1983. It's precious."

And with that, she started a pile of priceless treasures she was going to save. Into the pile went old sweat socks from Nathan's last football game, still unwashed. Then a broken rocker she used to sing the kids to sleep in when they were babies. On the pile, she put a tattered teddy bear, a dismembered Barbie doll, school backpacks, a wobbly skate board, rusting camping gear and once-used birthday candles. She added a pirate's mask from Halloween, broken squirt guns, a bird's nest that fell out of a tree one of the boys had given her.

When my wife was done, she had removed nearly everything from the garage sale to her pile. All that was left was my stuff — some rusting old golf clubs my father had taught me the game on, a hammock I received for Father's Day years ago but never got to use, baseball trophies from the kids' teams I used to coach, and a box full of old Star Wars toys I somehow missed in my clean sweep days.

I collected everything up and put it all on her pile. Then I went out to the street and stuck up a sign that read, "Garage sale canceled. Our memories aren't for sale anymore."

*At VMI, we don't have to worry about some crazy bringing a gun to school. The college gives everyone their own gun. Then they get a bayonet.*

# SURVIVING VMI

Our youngest son, Matt, went away to college four years ago and became a Rat. That's the affectionate term they give first year students at Virginian Military Institute in Lexington, Va.

As a Rat, he got to have his head shaved for six months, participate in 2 a.m. "sweat parties" to make him physically fit, and march in parades while living in a 130-year-old fortress that looks like a prison. He also carried a full college load.

Founded before the Civil War, VMI is what you would call a school with traditions. Students live four to a room, have no phones, no televisions, and the bathrooms are out the door and down the open tiers that line the four-story barracks. It's a spartan life at VMI. Beds at VMI are wooden cots with a two inch mattress. You have to roll up your bed — called a "hay" — in the morning and put it away. But, the cadets do have electricity and running water.

From the first day I saw VMI, I wondered why anyone would want to go to college there. My son apparently saw something different.

I'll never forget Matt's entry to VMI. His mother, Madeline, and I took him down to school in late summer for orientation, or, as cadets laughingly call it "hell week." On the first day, 380 male students plus all their parents assemble in this beautiful old chapel where school officers made speeches about honor, integrity and VMI brotherhood. They told us how Stonewall Jackson taught at VMI, and how George Marshall of the Marshall Plan, was a cadet there. Then they took our children away and shaved their heads.

## OUR SON THE RAT

The next time we see Matt, eight weeks later, he is bald, in uniform and marching in a parade. He is a "Rat."

A Rat is the lowest life form at VMI, parents are informed. Rats don't become cadets there until they survive six months of physical and mental "reconstruction" by the upperclassman. Matt and his peers have the privilege of being in the last "all-male rat line" at VMl because the school is to go coed the next year.

In addition to the bald head and military carriage Matt is now displaying, there are other changes in him as well. For example, he says strange things like "Sir" and "Ma'am" when he addresses us. At home, he could be a bit messy, but now he keeps his room spotless, his shoes polished and does his homework. Is this our child, we wonder?

VMI provides certain parental benefits you don't get at most colleges. For one, you always know where your children are because Rats can't leave campus the first year and have to be in their rooms by 11 p.m. They get "adopted" by local families who have them over for Sunday dinner and videos. Rats, who can be challenged to do things at any time by anyone on campus, suddenly discover they love church, where no one can touch them. They start going several times a week. Sometimes, they go to church several times a day.

Although his mother cries for him, we feel Matt is safe there. Madeline and I discover that even though we're 780 miles away, other Rat parents will take care of our son when we're not there. It's part of the unwritten code. Parents take other Rats out. A typical Rat weekend is 1) watching them parade 2) shopping at Wal-Mart, 3) eating anywhere and 4) letting them sleep in your hotel room. They get so little sleep between classes and work-outs, I actually saw one Rat doze off sitting straight up during a football game.

## DYKES AND BREAKOUT

The Rats all have "Dykes" during their first year. These are senior cadets, who show them the ropes, offer their rooms as sanctuary, and become an adviser and friend.  Somewhere in the continual grind of classes, daily physical discipline, 2 a.m. wake-up calls and bad cafeteria food, a real bonding occurs among the cadets. They become Brother Rats.

They learn the VMI honor code. You don't lie, cheat or steal, and the word "integrity" has meaning.

Six months after they start, on a cold blustery February day, Matt and the Rats "break out" of their confinement by climbing, en masse, a hill that has been turned into a wall of mud.  The school doesn't encourage parents to attend this event. There are no parade here.

The upperclassmen alternately hold back and help the Rats climb the muddy hill.  This final challenge has some message about life. As parents, we are never prouder than when we see a picture of Matt covered in muck from head-to-foot, smiling because he has survived the Rat Year and earned the privilege to be a VMI cadet. There are now 55 fewer cadets than when he started.

## THE VMI EXPERIENCE

As the years roll on, we discover the uniqueness of VMI. Parents of students become friends as we feed and entertain each other's cadets. We go to "Parents' Weekend," with tailgate parties stacked with southern hospitality. There are more parades. Strangers stop me in airports when I wear my VMI sweaters and ask what "Rat Class" I was in.

The cadets in their third year get the VMI ring, which has the history of the school on one side and the history of their Rat year on the other. It also holds a large stone in the center. The ring is as big as a golf ball.

Matt goes from "Rat" to "Rat with a Radio" to "Dyke with Rats." He takes a year off and attends Michigan State, where he discovers what real college life is like. He has fun, finds a girlfriend. He thinks about not going back but does, because he promised a Brother Rat he would.

# VMI NEVER FORGETS

While Matt's away, VMI accepts women to the ranks for the first time in its 150-year history. The school builds them separate washrooms, gives them guns and they learn to march in parades. One concession for female cadets. They can keep an inch of hair as Rats. We all think they'd look better bald.

Each year, Matt earns rank until he's a Lieutenant with his own troop which he leads in parades with a sword, sash and a feather plume hat. The four years have been filled with hardship, but also pride, joy and some sorrow.

Matt's best friend, Nathan Kowrach from St. Joseph, Mich., a buddy from grade school, goes with him to VMI and dies in his sleep at the end of his Rat year. In a dress uniform designed in 1870, Matt stands in an honor guard for his friend at the funeral. His Brother Rats buy Nate's class ring for him and 24 cadets come to Michigan to present it to his parents. The Class of 2000 ring has their son's initials on it with a cross. He's part of its history. VMI remembers its own.

A few weeks ago, our son Matt graduated with distinction from VMI. His Rats from Michigan are there. His Dyke, Eric, and a hundred other Dykes from four years ago come to see their "Rats" graduate. The school gives the graduates one final parade in their honor. The Class of 2000 has dwindled to just 240. At the end of the ceremony, the class is given its final order, "You are dismissed." Hats go flying up into the air. The "Ratline" brothers hug and congratulate each other. The parents cheer. Our cadets are now VMI grads.

After four years, it's over. Our son has gotten a unique education and we have 5,000 pictures of parades. I hate to say it, but I think I'm going to miss the place.

# Chapter 9
## SURVIVING THE HOLIDAYS

*From New Year's Day to Yom Kippur, the year is full of holidays that come with rituals and requirements from the stringing of outdoor Christmas lights to selecting the perfect Valentine's Day gift for your special love. Each has pitfalls for the unwary so be careful and watch out for Easter Bunny attacks.*

*This year I've decided that if I am going to make*
*New Year's resolutions they are going to be*
*more realistic and attainable.*

# SURVIVING NEW YEAR'S RESOLUTIONS

Like most people, I start out every year with a host of New Year's Resolutions that seem practical on paper but are really totally unrealistic and unattainable by most human standards.

My typical resolutions in the past have gone something like this:

"I resolve to stop all intake of food for the next 90 days, consuming only water, vitamins, and a few wilted carrot sticks so I can drop 30 pounds and regain the same weight I was the year that I resolved to lose 20 pounds by drinking Slim Fast as a dietary replacement for real food."

Or, I'll write down as a new year's goal:

"I resolve to exercise every day, seven days a week, for at least two hours a day, until the fat comes dripping off my body in puddles of sweat and I have achieved the muscular body tone I had when I was 20 years old."

Another annual goal I've often set for myself has been to become a better organized person. My annual goal usually looks like this:

"I resolve to set out a daily, weekly, and monthly plan of activities that will identify all of the work and home activities that need to be accomplished and complete those tasks on a pre-set schedule."

What usually happens after I make these resolutions is that two days into the new year, I am weak from hunger and ready to eat a sofa cushion, which I have done on occasion since there are no real calories in sofa cushions except for the stuff spilled on them that gets into the material.

# GIVE ME ONE OF EVERYTHING

The diet goes out the door by Jan. 4 every year when my car—for some unexplainable reason—will suddenly take on a life of its own and force me to hit the McDonald's drive-thru window where all dieting willpower disappears and I tell the lady at the window to "give me one of everything you've got."

As for exercise, I'll stay on a workout plan, for, oh, maybe three or four times and then start finding excuses why I can't go to the gym. Reasons like "It's too cold out" or "It's too hot out" or "My back hurts" or "My back doesn't hurt, but I don't want to hurt it exercising" or "I've just eaten everything they make at McDonald's and I'm too full to move."

As for getting organized, that hardly ever lasts past the first day, when I oversleep and it throws off my whole schedule for the next two weeks and I go back to my old habit of doing the project that has the highest priority of the overdue projects.

This year I've decided that if I am going to make new year's resolutions they are going to be more realistic and attainable. So, here are my new attainable resolutions.

## REALISTIC RESOLUTIONS

1. I resolve to eat anything I want, any time I want without care or concern about calories and how much weight it might put on me. I will also buy and wear clothes that are several sizes too big for me, so it looks like I'm losing weight.

2. I plan to put exercise into my daily schedule where ever and when ever practical and consistent to my life-style. For example, if my car should run out of gas and it's three miles to the nearest service station and it is a nice day, that's not too hot or too cold, I will walk to the station and back for the gas rather than send my wife out to get it.

3. I will always fill the car up when it is at the half tank level instead of waiting until the low gas light comes on, so I won't have to go out and walk three miles to a service station when I run out of gas.

4. I will get more organized during the new year and accomplish all the daily goals I set out to do. If I don't accomplish them during that day then I will move them into the next day or the next week.

5. I resolve to save more money by putting at least 20 percent of my paycheck into a savings plan. I will accomplish this by putting all of my purchases on credit cards and when those are full, I'll take out a home equity loan to pay off the cards. I will also count all those discounts I save on sale merchandise and spend that too.

6. I will read more books and do other mental exercises daily to help improve my memory which has been getting a little fuzzy in the past year. The nice thing about this resolution is that if I don't do it, I won't remember it anyway, so I won't feel bad about not doing it.

7. I resolve to do all of those unfinished household fix-up jobs that I have been putting off for years. I will do this as soon as I remember where I put the list of things to do.

8. I resolve to buy a very large giraffe and keep it in my garage. I don't really plan on doing this, I just thought I'd throw it in to see if you were still paying attention.

9. I will make more time to play ball and have quality time with my sons. Now all I need to do is get on their appointment calendars so we can schedule these activities.

10. I resolve to smile more at people I meet and have a lot more fun during the new year. Now, there is a resolution I believe I can keep.

*Many guys make the mistake of giving their girlfriends
diamond engagement rings on Valentine's Day.
Sure, it's romantic, but what do you
do for an encore?*

# SURVIVING VALENTINE'S DAY

Think quick, guys. Valentine's Day is four days away. Your girlfriend, wife, significant other is expecting something really romantic and sentimental from you on this day. What do you do?

If you're like most guys, you're probably right now going "Wow, four days until Valentine's Day. That's great, I thought it was last weekend." Then you'll wait until the last minute and show up at her door with some plastic roses, which glow in the dark, that you bought at the Shell gas station.

And after she expresses wide-eyed amazement at your plastic flowers, she'll hide in the bathroom sobbing while you stand outside the door going, "What? What'd I do now?"

Not that this has ever happened to me. But I hear stories like this from other men. Guys standing around the water cooler the morning after Valentine's Day going, "Can you image that, $7.50 right down the drain. I would have been better off buying that chrome gas cap for my car."

But there's hope. You still have time this year to make yourself a sensitive kind of Valentine's Day guy and turn what could be the most miserable day in your life into a happy occasion. All you have to do is follow these rules.

### VALENTINE'S DAY RULES FOR MEN

1) Always remember Valentine's Day. It's simple, the day always falls on February 14. You should have that date tattooed on your arm.

2) Women like flowers. Tattoo that right under "February 14."

3) Roses are the best flowers to give on Valentine's Day. Stay away from things like tulips, lilies and wisteria, even though they may seem pretty to you.

If you buy roses, be careful. Roses send a message even if you don't know what it is. Here are the rules.

a) A single rose means you care.

b) Giving her up to three roses means you care three times as much and are extremely thoughtful.

c) A dozen roses says you're crazy in love.

d) Anything in between three and a dozen roses, though, says you're too cheap to fork out for the whole dozen and she'll walk around for the next two months wondering why you don't love her.

4) Order the roses from a florist and have them delivered. Delivery is very important. Don't ask me why. My florist gave me that advice and he's a smart guy because he's very rich from delivering all those roses on Valentine's Day.

If you can't afford florist-delivered roses, then buy the flowers yourself and give them to her when you are alone in a romantic setting. But if you're going to buy your own roses, remember this: Roses from the Shell station usually smell like motor fuel. Better to buy them at a grocery store, just don't give them to her in a brown paper shopping bag. Plastic is always preferable. Add that to your tattoo.

## TATOO LIST

To summarize, your tattoo so far should read:

February 14, Valentine's Day
Buy Flowers— no wisteria
1 Rose — you care
3 roses— you care a lot
6 Roses — you cheapskate
12 Roses — you wonderful guy
No roses from gas stations
Plastic not paper

## ADVANCED VALENTINE'S DAY TRAINING

After you've mastered flower purchasing, the next level is the Valentine's Day card. Yes, I realize you just spent all your poker money on the roses, but without a Valentine's Day card to go with them, you're a bum. Don't ask me why. Those are the rules. So here's a few tips on selecting a Valentine's Day card.

It should have the color red and a picture of a heart on the card. It should also contain words that say how you feel about her like "love, treasure, you, devotion, special and Valentine's Day."

Whatever you do, never buy a Valentine's Day card that you think is cute and clever that reads "Happy Valentine's Day, Gone Bowling, See you later." Bad boy. Put that card down.

Also, beware of buying candy for your special lady on Valentine's Day. Candy can be very tricky. I know you're probably saying to yourself, "Hey, candy is a good idea. It's a gift I can enjoy, too," but don't do it. You'll either wind up eating too much and she'll feel you bought her candy so you could eat it (they notice these things), or she'll eat most of it herself, gain weight and blame it on you.

## BRIGHT SHINING THINGS

Another gift you want to be careful about giving on Valentine's Day, guys, is small, bright shining things, and I'm not talking about fishing lures. I mean rings.

Many guys make the mistake of giving their girlfriends diamond engagement rings on Valentine's Day. Sure, it's romantic, but what do you do for an encore? So, you come back the next year and give her a single rose and she'll go, "He doesn't love me any more. Last year, he gave me a diamond on Valentine's Day and this year all I got was a lousy dead flower smelling of gasoline."

So, for a happy future with the one you love, follow my advice and add these things to your tattoo.

Buy cards — nice words

No candy

Start small and work up

Don't explain this tattoo.

*The Easter Bunny was just a mythical creature that most kids believed would bring them chocolate candy and eggs on Easter. Except in my house.*

# SURVIVING EASTER BUNNY ATTACKS

The Easter Bunny came to our house the other night. Sometime between midnight and dawn, it broke in and left a pink, blue and green Easter Bunny tree in our living room.

The tree is about 2 feet high and decorated with bunnies, Easter eggs, carrots and something that looks like Donald Duck with his feet stuck in a bucket of cement. It's the type of Easter holiday decoration that I'll want to treasure and pass on to our children, which is something I'm planning to do next week.

My first thought, though, when I saw the thing was, "What is that doing here?" I must have also said those words out loud as well as thinking them, because my wife, Madeline, got kind of defensive suddenly.

"That's an Easter Tree," she said, explaining the meaning of all the cute things hanging from the tree's pastel limbs. "The Easter Bunny must have brought it."

While my wife may have thought the idea of a furry marauder sneaking into our house in the middle of the night, skulking around silently while we lay sleeping, was cute, the image brought shivers to my spine.

You see, I do not have the same warm and cuddly childhood memories of the Easter Bunny as most people. Mine are quite horrifying.

### THE EASTER BUNNY MONSTER

When I was a kid, we didn't have the chance like kids today to meet the Easter Bunny and sit on his lap at the mall. For one thing, we didn't have malls in those days, and so the Easter Bunny was just a mythical creature kids believed would bring them chocolate candy and eggs on Easter. Except in my house.

Back in the 1950s, when I was about 5 years old, I naively asked my older brother, Stan, how the Easter Bunny came into being. My brother told me that the Easter Bunny was created as the result of an unauthorized government experiment with atomic radiation that changed the molecular structure of a common rabbit so that it grew to gigantic proportions, was able to fly and breathe fire.

"You know, just like Godzilla," he said, seriously, passing on this bit of wisdom to his younger brother.

Ever since that day, I lived in fear of the Easter Bunny. Weeks before Easter, I used to imagine a 60-foot-tall Easter Bunny coming to attack our little town, trampling its homes and street cars under furry rabbit feet while lobbing 8-foot Easter eggs like mortar shells at our municipal buildings. I would have nightmares where I'd wake up from a deep sleep and there would be this giant pink eye peeking in through my bedroom window at me.

My brother didn't help, of course. Before bed, Stan would terrorize me with stories of giant bloody bunny tracks being found in the field beside our house. He also told me how someone's pet collie was discovered encased in a 5-foot-high pile of bunny droppings. The dog was alive, but now would run in terror at the sight of even baby bunnies.

Then, to make matters worse, Hollywood brought out the movie "Night of the Lapin," in which civilization comes under attack from giant mutated bunnies who munch on unwary humans. My brother took me to see it and told me it was a documentary.

He once had a friend show up at our house with the sleeve of a bloody shirt ripped off and his arm missing. The two of them told me that a giant rabbit had bit his arm off. I didn't even catch on when his friend grew his arm back several days later. My brother just said it was a result of the atomic poisoning in the rabbit's blood.

# EASTER PARADE TERROR

And why shouldn't I believe my brother about the Easter Bunny? He's the same person who warned me about vampires, werewolves and zombies that lived in our neighborhood and came out at night to hunt.

To say the least, I lived in terror at the expected coming of the Easter Bunny. I couldn't understand why other children were so happily looking forward to his annual visit.

My fear was so great, I once passed out in terror when my parents took me to an Easter parade and a giant bunny balloon appeared from around the corner. And I avoided Easter egg hunts in those days like the plague, imagining the wanton devastation a berserk 60-foot Easter Bunny could reek on innocent children lured to an open field in the quest of Easter eggs.

But there was a way to protect yourself. My brother told me the only way to stop an Easter Bunny attack was to hang crucifixes made out of blessed palms in your windows and walk backward for seven days. So, while other kids were out frolicking in the sun the week before Easter, I spent my childhood warding off giant Easter Bunny attacks by braiding crosses and tripping over things I couldn't see because I was walking backward.

I guess I had forgotten these things over the years, blanked them out from my conscious mind until I saw the Easter Bunny tree sitting in my living room. All of the terror of the lost days of my youth came flooding back to me as I began inching away from the bunny tree.

"What's wrong?" my wife asked. "Don't you like it?"

"No, it's fine," I said, walking out of the room backward while looking over my shoulder. "I just have to go braid some crosses now."

*I remember asking the nurse when our first son was born, "Do
I put his feet on my shoulder with the head hanging down,
or is it the other way around?"*

# SURVIVING FATHERHOOD

This Sunday is Father's Day, one of those annual events
that the funny tie makers and greeting card companies look forward to all year long.

But Father's Day is more than just opening up boxes with
loud shirts bearing 34 different brands of beer on it that you might
have worn when you were a swinging single, but looks a little
out of place at your kids' parent-teacher conferences. Especially
when the teacher goes "Oh, yes, Mr. Budweiser, little Johnnie is
doing real well in school. He can count all the way up to 100
bottles of beer on the wall."

Being a father really starts when guys who can catch a
40-yard spiral pass one-handed in touch football, or deftly sink a
hoop on the run from the three-point line, turn into fumbling
mutants when handed the little bundle of joy that is their child.

I remember asking the nurse when our first son was born,
"Do I put his feet on my shoulder with the head hanging down,
or is it the other way around?" This happens because guys don't
get the baby training women do while they are growing up.

## BABY COUSIN BOWLING

Back when I was young and there was a birth in our ex-
tended family, all of my girl cousins would get excited with the
new baby and fuss over it and want to hold the little tyke and
change its diaper and watch it make faces. The boy cousins would
just look at the new baby in wonder for about three seconds and
then go, "Wow. Can we take the baby bowling?"

I was 8 when that happened and it was probably the last
time I saw or held a newborn — we all had to hold the baby and

have our pictures taken with the new cousin without dropping him — until my own children started coming along.

As you can imagine, I was terrified when our first son, Jason, was born. Don't get me wrong, I wasn't afraid of the kid. He was only about 5 1/2 pounds and I figured I could take him the best two out of three rounds any time. No, I was terrified that my wife, Madeline, might leave me alone with him and he'd start crying because he wanted something and I wouldn't be able to decipher what he wanted.

As a guy, I just couldn't understand what the baby wanted when he cried. At least, not like my wife could. She intuitively understood every cry and whimper our new son made. Jason would cry and she'd go, "Oh, he's hungry" or "He's wet" or "He has a burp stuck and wants to be placed on his stomach and patted on the back."

But I learned. I'd be alone with the baby and he would start crying and I'd call to my wife and say, "Honey, the baby's crying. I think he wants you."

Things got a little easier when our second son, Nathan, came along. By then, I had learned that you don't toss newborns way up in the air and try to catch them. They don't like that at all and usually start to cry and you have to go "Honey, the baby needs his mother." But by then, Madeline too had a better understanding of babies and whenever I did that, she would say, "No, I think he's crying for his father."

## UNDERSTANDING A CHILD'S NEEDS

Gradually, as time passed, I came to understand the needs of my children better, especially once they began to talk. I became adept at understanding their cute baby talk phrases. When our child would say, "I want something to eat, Dad. I'm starving," I knew it meant "give me numnums," and I would respond with, "Here's a Snickers bar, but don't tell your mother."

By the time Matt, our third son arrived, I was an old pro with babies. I could feed him, change him, burp him and understand his little cries.

Matt would go "Waaaaa…Waaaaa…" and I'd say "What? You want to go to the ice cream store for an ice cream cone? You got it, pal."

Through the raising of our three sons, I also learned what being a father is all about. It's realizing you've helped bring a life into the world that is part of you and will always be a part of you. It's sharing their childhood joys and sorrows and, when you can, making it all better.

It's keeping them close at hand when they're small, and letting them go on their own when they're ready. It's making sure they stay on the straight and narrow when they're in sight, but trusting them to do it on their own when you're not around.

Fatherhood is teaching them the fine art of baseball and football until the are better than you and you don't mind it. It's watching them glow with delight at discovering things you've long forgotten. It's being with them when they need you to hold the bike steady as they learn to ride, then letting go when it's time for them to ride alone.

Fatherhood is balancing motherhood. Letting your children try the things they're too young to do, but ready to try. It's worrying about them when they're sick and worrying about them when they're healthy. It's also watching them grow and develop into their own person. Someone you helped shape.

What I've learned about fatherhood over these many years while, my children grew, is that Father's Day is every day.

*"Let's have lasagna for Thanksgiving," I suggested.*
*"We always have turkey on Thanksgiving.*
*I think we're in a rut."*

# SURVIVING THANKSGIVING DINNER

It's Thanksgiving today. The one day of the year when all Americans sit down and eat the same thing for dinner.

If you stop to think about it, that's an amazing thing. I mean, the government couldn't pass a law forcing us to all eat the same meal once a year.

I can hear the complaints now if they tried. "There go those politicians again. Can't decide on who's the president, but they're going to tell us what we have to eat today," people would say, and then go cook up some Spam or something.

This year, I thought our household should try something different for a change.

"Let's have lasagna for Thanksgiving," I suggested. "We always have turkey on Thanksgiving. I think we're in a rut."

My family looked at me as if I had gone insane.

"Or how about pizza? You know, something different this year," I said to a chorus of boos. They're all such traditionalists.

## TRADITIONAL THANKSGIVING

Actually, historians believe it is more likely that the Pilgrims and the Native Americans ate venison that first Thanksgiving rather than turkey. It seems deer were easier to hunt because they made bigger targets than wild turkeys, which could move through brush faster than the Road Runner.

The Pilgrims were known to say: "Did you get us a turkey for dinner, John Smith?"

"No," Smith would reply. "Just another eight-point buck."

I can imagine what Thanksgiving would be like around our house today if we had adopted eating deer on Thanksgiving instead of turkey.

For one thing, a whole deer takes a lot more stuffing.

"I'll need 50 loaves of bread and two pounds of sage for that deer," says my wife, mulling over her stuffing recipe.

Trying to get a full-grown deer in our tiny oven would be a chore, too.

"I told you to cut off the antlers, Mom," says our youngest son, Matthew.

I'd need a chain saw to carve the beast.

"Who wants a leg?" I ask, chain saw in hand.

Then, there would be the problem of what do you do with 130 pounds of leftovers.

"Not deer hash again," the kids would protest after Thanksgiving.

"Be quiet and eat your dinner. We've almost finished the Thanksgiving deer," my wife, Madeline, would state in July.

I guess it could be worse. Historians also believe that squirrel was part of the first Thanksgiving feast, as well as fresh pigeon.

Just imagine what it would be like if we had these foods for Thanksgiving dinner instead of turkey. It would probably go something like: "I'm sorry kids, there's no Thanksgiving pigeon this year," my wife tells the children. "You're father put it on a cracker and it's all gone.

"But there's plenty of squirrel left," she says brightly.

## BRING ON THE BADGER

And still it could have been worse than that. Badger was also a delicacy in Pilgrim times. They say it tastes like chicken. Or, at least muskrat.

Imagine Thanksgiving with a badger for dinner.

"Honey, would you check the oven," my wife calls to me. "I think the badger's almost done."

Now, how do you gauge when a badger is thoroughly cooked? There's no setting on the microwave for badger. And the oven thermometer only goes up to opossum.

"Let's see," I would muse. " A 10-pound badger, minus fur, is probably equivalent to a five-pound chuck roast."

When  the badger was done, we'd call everyone to the table  and I'd begin to carve.

"Who wants the snout?" I'd ask. "Anyone for a leg? There's four of them."

All things considered, I guess we are lucky that our forefathers in their wisdom chose the turkey for our Thanksgiving meal.  So on this day, when we give thanks for all the blessing we have received during the year, let us also salute the noble turkey that graces our dining room table and say: "Gobble, gobble."

*We inherited the tradition of decorating outdoor trees, bushes and the tops of houses from my wife's side of the family. My father never budged from his stance that Christmas lights belonged on the inside of the house, preferably on the tree.*

# SURVIVING CHRISTMAS LIGHTS

My wife informed me the other day that it's time to take down the Halloween decorations and put up the outdoor Christmas lights.

Even before she mentioned it, I could tell we were approaching the annual Christmas light decorating day, because the temperature had started dropping toward freezing and snow clouds began filling the sky.

Why I can't put up Christmas tree lights in July or August, when it's warm outside and safe to go up on the roof, is beyond me. Besides, the ground is softer when I fall.

But my wife says it doesn't matter what the season, a fall from our roof would probably kill me any way.

With that reassuring thought, I head out for my destiny. As I carry away the frozen carcasses of this year's Halloween pumpkins, they seem to laugh at me with their frozen smiles as I haul them off to the compost heap. Their job is done, mine has just begun.

We inherited the tradition of decorating outdoor trees, bushes and the tops of houses from my wife's side of the family. My father, wise man that he was, never budged from his stance that Christmas lights belonged on the inside of the house, preferably on the tree.

So like my father-in-law before me, putting up the exterior Christmas lights fell to the oldest male of the household.

I've tried to get my three boys interested in it over the years to no avail. My oldest son claims he hates outdoor lights and refuses to come out of his room until the lights are up. Then he comes out to admire them. My middle son, since he was a youngster, is always sick or has football injuries that prevent him from moving during daylight. And the youngest, even as a toddler, claimed he had vertigo and got nose bleeds from heights.

I had often thought of adopting another son to help me, but adoption agencies refused to even consider my Christmas light decorating need as a viable consideration for adoption.

## AESTHETIC ENLIGHTENMENT

So each year, I face the task alone. Well, not quite alone. My wife is there beside me to provide styling assistance to my endeavors. It seems the aesthetic placement of the lights falls to the female head of the house in my wife's family. Unfortunately, this does not include any physical assistance.

"I think I'd like to hang a star on the top of the pine tree this year," she says, pointing to the top of a 40-foot Norwegian pine in our yard.

"No one will see the star on top of the tree but birds and low-flying aircraft," I protest.

"But it will shine on them for the holidays," she responds.

I've learned from experience, there is no arguing with that kind of logic. So for the next two months, squirrels, magpies and our neighbor's second-floor bedroom window will receive the holiday magic of our unblinking Christmas star.

Actually, the task of putting up outside Christmas decorations has become easier over the years. I just never take down last year's lights. But that doesn't keep me from having to climb up and add new lines in previously undiscovered nooks and crannies of the house.

The problem today is that Christmas lights are too cheap. In the old days, a string of lights cost $7 and you got 12 lights on a line. Nowadays you get 6,000 lights for about $5.99. My wife actually feels guilty if we don't go out and buy a couple thousand of those tiny little lights each December.

"But they burn out like leaves in a fire," I protest.

"So what," she says. "There's thousands of more where they came from."

Every year, we get more and more lights for me to hang up right over the lifeless strands of Christmas past. Burned out light strings around our place hang down from trees like green tendrils of jungle vine. Small children swing on them in the summer time.

## EVERGREEN LIGHTNING RODS

The mass of Christmas light wiring strung around our rooftop has turned our house into a virtual radio telescope, which allows us to track deep space pulsars like NASA. Our evergreen trees are lightning rods in electrical storms. And still I string up more light.

Actually, the easiest lights for me to put up are the backyard display lights. What? You mean everybody doesn't decorate trees in their back yard, trees that only me and the dog and the gas man ever get to see?

Not only do I decorate trees in the back yard, somehow I've got the job of creating Christmas scenes out of the tiny, white light strings. Of course, we couldn't do anything simple like go out and buy one of those ready-made light sculptures of Santa and his reindeer or the Macy's Christmas parade. Nooooo. I've got to make ours from scratch.

But, like I said, these are the easiest Christmas lights I put up. I just go out in the back yard and throw up a bunch of lines in the trees and then that night, with the family gathered around, turn them on to see what I've created.

The first year I did this, the lights made the perfect image of a group of angels singing hymns. A true Christmas miracle if I ever saw one.

Since then, I've just left the lights up and added to them randomly each year. The second year they were up, the angel image — left dangling through the winds of winter, spring snow and summer heat — transformed itself magically into the nativity scene at Bethlehem. I was a hero. A Christmas light artist.

The next year, with the addition of a few lines of lights, the scene changed to Santa's workshop, then a Dickens Christmas with Tiny Tim and Scrooge.

But, I knew my string of luck with the lights would eventually run out. This year, when I turned on the lights to see what wonder I had created, the lights looked exactly like a Japanese movie monster.

"Daddy," cried my youngest in terror. "Godzilla ate our Christmas decorations."

"No, that's just a big Christmas puppy with fangs, stepping on Tokyo," I assured them.

They just looked at me like I was out of my mind, tears welling up in their eyes.

"I'll go get more lights," I said, and headed for the house.

# Chapter 10
# SURVIVING CHRISTMAS

*If you haven't guessed, this chapter is devoted to Christmas and helpful advice ranging from buying the perfect present — never get sucked into buying your wife a vacuum sweeper for Christmas — to surviving Christmas shopping. The thing to remember about Christmas is the good memories that stay in your heart long after the day is gone.*

*Sometimes, I think strangers just pick our names off the Eddie Bauer catalog list and send us these holiday letters to brag about how well they are doing.*

# SURVIVING HOLIDAY LETTERS

I love getting Christmas letters from friends. Everyone always has so much wonderful news to write about. Their letters are so full of great achievements and wonderful things that have happened to them during the year that when I read them, I stop to wonder what I'm doing wrong with my life. The other day we got a holiday letter from Babs and Lars that went like this:

\*\*\*\*\*\*\*\*

Dear friends and loved ones,

We will always remember this as the year we took a wonderful, free trip to the British Isles and saw England, Scotland and Wales. We had nothing but beautiful, sunny days as we visited cities, cathedrals and famous sites we'll never forget.

Our son, Gunther, is now a senior at Notre Dame where he is majoring in astrophysics and philosophy while he holds down a full-time volunteer job helping underprivileged children. He is lettering in four varsity sports and just received notice he has been named to the National Academic Research Center for Intelligent School Seniors In Science Technology (NARCISSIST) for finding a cure for athlete's foot.

Our daughter, Justine, has been selected valedictorian of her class while still a junior. She is interested in music and electronics, and recently completed building her own viola and electric guitar synthesizer for a class project that earned her a full scholarship to any college in the world.

Lars has been named president of his bank after starting as a teller last year. And I've taken up the cause of Mother Teresa in between consulting assignments to the White House, while ghostwriting my third housekeeping tips book for Martha Stewart.

Love, Babs, Lars & Family

The funny thing about this letter is we don't even know these people. Sometimes, I think strangers just pick our names off the Eddie Bauer catalog list and send us these holiday letters to brag about how well they are doing.

Our own holiday letter is usually a little more down to earth. Here's a sample of this year's family newsletter, which we will have finished and mailed by some time in February or March.

\*\*\*\*\*\*\*\*\*\*\*

Hi Folks,
Well, not much happened this year. Write soon.
Just us.
\*\*\*\*\*\*\*\*\*\*\*

Actually that was just the first draft. Here's how it really turned out.
\*\*\*\*\*\*\*\*\*\*\*

Hi Gang,
Well, this year started out like it usually does around here with January kicking off the year. Our youngest son, Matt, completed his first year of military college at Virginia Military Institute where they made him live in a cellblock with 1,300 other guys. They yelled at him 24 hours a day, made him make his bed every morning, deprived him of television and made him say "Yes Sir, and No Ma'am" to everyone. He loved it. If his mom and I had tried to do this when he was home, we'd have been accused of child abuse.

Our middle son, Nathan, is now a seventh-year junior at Michigan State University. He's only 147 credits away from getting his degree in art/history/business/psychology/science/literature/education. He plans on getting a job in a rock band when he's done.

Actually, he graduated this spring and is just completing his teacher's training. And now, if he'll let me out of this head lock, I'll finish this letter.

197

Jay, our oldest son, has his Elvis impersonation down to a tee and is looking to take his act to Vegas this year. We really don't mind him wearing the cape around the house, but do object to having to call him "The King" all the time.

Madeline is still principal of a 600-student elementary school, which is bigger than some of the school districts she's taught in. One of her little students this year told her, they shouldn't be calling her a prince-a-pal. The student said, "You're a lady, they should call you a princess-a-pal."

We got into some home improvement things this year. Myron put tile in the kitchen. He decided to do it himself after finding out it would cost $700 for an expert to do the job. Instead, it cost us $5,000 for the carpal tunnel surgery he had to have on both his wrists, elbows and knees after he was finished.

For spring break, we went to the "Magic Kingdom" this year, but it was closed.

Myron almost won the million-dollar state lottery again. He had all the right numbers, but they were on a ticket for his laundry.

The highlight of our year once again was our summer vacation to Warsaw, Indiana, where we saw the world's largest ear of corn. As usual, our family reunion in July got washed out by flash flooding again this year. Luckily, we had put everything in the life rafts before the deluge and were able to finish the picnic 20 miles upstream.

Well, that's about it for this year. In this Holy Season, our wish for all of our dear friends and family is that each may find the secret to living each day with zest while finding happiness and joy in the simple things. May God keep you safe and give you many blessings in the new year and the strength to get through the sprinkling of life's difficult times when they come your way.

From the Kukla House to yours: HAPPY HOLIDAYS! MERRY CHRISTMAS! HAPPY HANUKKAH! HAPPY KWANZAA! And a Feliz Navidad to you all."

*Oh, how I envy those husbands whose wives have the foresight to do all of their Christmas shopping in July and have everything wrapped and under the tree before Labor Day.*

# SURVIVING CHRISTMAS SHOPPING

"I don't want to go to the mall again. I don't want to go to the mall again," came the wail from the front seat of my car.

But it wasn't a cranky, tired, little kid being dragged to one more store for Christmas shopping who was crying. It was a big cranky, tired husband who was making his 49th shopping trip since Thanksgiving creating all the noise.

"Don't be such a baby about it," said my wife, Madeline, patting my head and making me take my thumb out of my mouth so I could drive with both hands. "Besides, we'll only be there a few minutes. And if you're a good boy, I might buy you a hot chocolate."

While the hot chocolate sounded good, I knew from past experience being in the mall for just a "few minutes" was a big fib. That ploy wasn't true when my mother used it to drag my father to mall Christmas shopping and it won't be true when my great grandchildren get pulled out of a comfy chair from in front of a great football game for one more shopping spree on the 12th day before Christmas. Who do wives think they're kidding when they say stopping at the mall at Christmas will only take a few minutes? Everybody knows just finding a parking place at the mall this time of year, can take half an hour.

Oh, how I envy those husbands whose wives have the foresight to do all of their Christmas shopping in July and have everything wrapped and under the tree before Labor Day. My friend Deryk's wife, Helen, is like that. Deryk hasn't had to go to a mall for Christmas shopping since 1979. In fact, he's got it so good, that Helen even buys his presents for her while doing the Christmas shopping, thus saving any needless trip to the mall to return things after the holiday.

Granted this couple gets a lot of summer clothes for Christmas — halter tops, swim suits, beach towels, sandals, etc.— but it's the thought that counts.

## THE TINSEL RUNS

On the other hand, my wife and I seem to be out shopping during the Christmas season from morning to night, seven days a week. Every hour we're not working, sleeping or busy putting up the tree and house lights, we're at the mall.

Often, it's not even Christmas presents we're after when we go to the mall. We also make tinsel runs, string light replacement excursions, she-bought-me-a-gift-I've-got-to-get-her- something return trips as well as the once-in-a-lifetime-never-to-be-repeated-until-next-week 12-hour sales that also draws us.

Actually, I think I resent going to the mall — and I use the term "mall" generically to signify any store that sells you things — because, well, I always feel they're trying to sell me something. And they do it so early now, it's almost a crime.

I walked into one store at the mall this year the day after Halloween. Christmas music was playing and the whole place had been turned into a cheery winter wonderland complete with once- in-a-lifetime-never-to-be-repeated-until-next-week 12-hour holiday sale.

"Merry Christmas," cried the perky young saleswoman who greeted me as she finished putting Christmas lights on a Jack-O- Lantern that hadn't got packed away yet. "Are we out looking for that special Christmas gift for that certain someone?"

"Not yet," I replied, "unless that certain someone is dreaming of getting a leaf rake for Christmas," I replied. Instead I headed for the hardware department where I got a leaf rake, some garbage bags, and a quart of lawn mower oil, all of which the saleswoman gift-wrapped for me.

Along with the free gift wrapping, the store gave me a 30 percent off discount coupon with the garbage bags for any purchase made at the jewelry department. But the coupon was only good during the Christmas "Midnight Madness" sale which started that minute. The sale would be running until dawn, finishing just before the launch of the store's Christmas "Early Bird" shopping spree during which everything was going to be 40 percent off with the purchase of a leaf rake.

## SAVING MORE BY BUYING

I hate to say it but I succumbed to the marketing pressure and the Christmas music and spent the next 24 hours in the store doing Christmas shopping on the day after Halloween. I bought gifts for every person I could possibly think would want one, saving more and more money every time I made a purchase. In the middle of the buying frenzy I remember briefly thinking, "If I keep saving money like this, I'll be rich soon."

I mean I bought watches, and earrings, sleepwear and sweaters, intimate apparel, snowboards, backboards, washboards; you name it, I bought it. And I got them all gift wrapped for free. For the first time in my life I was done with my Christmas shopping two months before Christmas. This year there would be no last minute frenzied buying of leftover Iguana handbags for my wife — no more broken toys for my kids. This year I was done early. My friend Helen would be proud of me.

So, although all of my Christmas shopping is behind me this year, I still found myself being dragged to the mall for one more shopping trip. Is it any wonder I'm whiny and cranky and miserable?

"Now you just sit here and drink your hot chocolate dear and I'll be back in a few minutes," said my wife, leading me to a mall bench near the Santa booth before she disappeared for the rest of the day.

I have to admit it was quite pleasant sitting there with the hot chocolate, watching all the shoppers bustling about as Christmas songs played. At least I didn't have to fight all those people trying to buy gifts. My Christmas shopping is all done. And all I have to do now is remember where I put everything.

*My wife put on her Christmas list that she wanted a new vacuum sweeper. Now, I know better then to actually go out and buy her a sweeper. I've been sucked into that trap before.*

# SURVIVING CHRISTMAS GIFT BUYING

I looked at the calendar today and there are 14 shopping days left until Christmas. You would think that with two weeks to shop, I'd have all the time in the world to get out and buy those perfect gifts that will make this a Christmas to remember for the whole family. But, you'd be wrong.

What will happen is, I'll sit around thinking I've got all this time to shop, and then Christmas Eve, I'll wake up and realize I haven't bought a single present.

To prepare for my Christmas shopping, I usually have members of my family write out complete, detailed lists of things they want for Christmas. Once they turn their lists over to me, I promptly lose them until the day after Christmas. Since I can't ask them for another list, or they'll think I'm a complete klutz who can't hang on to a Christmas list, I usually have to wing it on the family presents.

If, by chance, I remember some of the things on their lists, instead of just buying the stuff right away, I walk through whole bunches of stores for days, trying to determine the best prices, colors and sizes of the things they want. Once I've done all my research, lost the list and wasted the 13 days before Christmas, I'll run out on Noel's Eve and pay through the nose for anything that remotely resembles what my wife and kids wanted.

This has led to some interesting presents over the years. Like the year my wife, Madeline, asked for an eel-skin wallet for Christmas and instead got a handbag that looked like an Iguana. Or, the Christmas my kids wanted the hand-held "Game Boy," but all I could remember was that it was something electronic and you pushed buttons. So, I got them a calculator.

# THE CROCK POT TRAP

It's my philosophy, that you can't just rush out and buy everything on a Christmas list. Some things are inappropriate.

For example, this year my wife put on her Christmas list that she wanted a new vacuum sweeper. Now, I know better than to actually go out and buy her a sweeper. I've been sucked into that trap before.

I remember one year when we were first married, Madeline had on her Christmas list an electric crock pot and gold hoop earrings. She told me that the earrings were just an afterthought, and what she really wanted was the crock pot so she could cook her family nutritious meals.

She told me numerous times over the weeks before Christmas that she "really, really" wanted that crock pot. So I bought it for her. On Christmas Day, when she opened her present, she cried, "I can't believe you bought me a crock pot for Christmas. Is that all I mean to you — a cook?"

"But ..." I stammered, stunned by her sudden change of heart. "That's what you said you wanted."

So, I don't get fooled by that one anymore. Any time she puts a household appliance on her Christmas gift list, whether it's a vacuum, sewing machine or electric fry pan, I immediately cross it off and replace it with gold hoop earrings.


# BUILD YOUR OWN PRESENT

Although most women don't want household appliances for Christmas —even if they say they do — wives think it's fine to buy us guys table saws, work benches and tools for Christmas. Somehow, women have the impression that men enjoy puttering around the house, building and fixing things instead of watching professional football, basketball and Frisbee on television in our spare time.

One year, I put on my Christmas list that I would like a cushy, reclining chair and maybe "one hammer." My wife got me a 298-piece tool set in a 3-foot tool box that weighed 60 pounds. I had enough tools to open my own hardware store. There was no sign of the reclining chair. I did, though, now have enough tools to build one myself.

Another thing I cross off my wife's  list every year is clothes. I learned that lesson one year when she asked for a sweater and I got her this beautiful black and orange Angora sweater with a discreet picture of the Grateful Dead on the front made out of beer cans. (The guys out there are going, "Hey, that sounds neat.") The salesperson who sold me the sweater said it was a "one-of-a-kind original that might go up in value." I think he was right, because Madeline has never taken it out of the box, and it's now stored away somewhere in our basement for safe keeping.

So, over the years, I've tended to play it safe and buy her mostly gold hoop earrings. She has about 20 sets right now. But this year, I thought I'd do something different. For months now, she's been complaining about allergies, and wishing I'd get all of the furnace duct work cleaned out.

So as a surprise this year, instead of the hoop earrings, I've scheduled a company to come in and do duct cleaning of our house on Christmas Eve as her present. She's going to love it, and the best part is, it's not a household appliance.

Am I clever or what?

*I tend to overeat at holiday gatherings because I'm just not aware that I am eating the equivalent of three times the daily nutritional requirements of a Sumo wrestler at these parties just in artichoke dip alone.*

## SURVIVING HOLIDAY PARTIES

I just got back from a holiday Christmas party where in a single evening I consumed about 6,000 calories disguised in the form of nacho chips, Jalapeño dip, Parmesan cheese bites, honey-pecan tarts and, of course, those little salami spirals made with cream cheese with an olive in the middle.

As I topped off my evening of holiday feasting with two spoonfuls of Pepto Abysmal, my darling wife asked ever so caringly, "Why on earth would you eat all those things?"

I thought about the question for a minute before responding to her question.

I didn't plan to eat all of that stuff. Really, who goes out saying to themselves "I'm going to eat everything that is not nailed down because it's the holidays and I have to."

It just happens.

First of all, you don't want to offend your host and hostess who have slaved for several days preparing homemade goodies, or, at least given a lot of thought to ordering everything from a caterer.

I would consider it bad manners not to sample a few sausage stuffed mushroom caps, which are really good and go very well with the pimento and garlic cheese dip that I pour on top.

At least, I think I was supposed to pour the garlic dip on top. It tasted good that way. In fact, after they ran out of the stuffed mushroom caps I found the garlic cheese dip was even better on the oatmeal and raisin cookies that were sitting nearby. A word of advice, though, don't put garlic cheese dip on raspberry-almond tarts. It is just not a good blend of flavors.

# NOT EVERYDAY FOOD

The thing about holiday parties is that you just don't get this kind of food everyday at home. I mean how many times a week do you eat shrimp puffs for dinner? Or plum-glazed chicken tidbits? And when was the last time at home you were able to sample Key Lime pie, pecan pie and a double chocolate tort on the same plate.

Actually, I had all those pastries on one plate just a couple weeks ago at Thanksgiving, but that's not the point. The point is none of us eat like this every day, so when the opportunity presents itself like at the holidays, I indulge.

The other reason I tend to overeat at holiday gatherings is because I'm just not aware that I am eating the equivalent of three times the daily nutritional requirements of a Sumo wrestler at these parties just in artichoke dip alone.

You know how these things go. I'm at the buffet table with an old friend I haven't seen since the last Christmas party and I'm talking, I'm eating, I'm eating, I'm talking. Eventually, I push myself away from the buffet table ( Hey, nobody told me I wasn't supposed to sit there.) and I go off to some other part of the house to get away from the food.

But, there is no escape from the food at these parties. No matter where I go in the house there is food. I go stand by the fireplace in hopes the heat will burn off a few of the pounds I just ingested and there on the mantle piece is a bowl of chocolate covered cherries. I think to myself "the heat is going to melt them. I better save them from that terrible fate."

I flee from the chocolate cherries and go to the family room and there sit 12 bowls of peanuts, chips, dips, salsa, chocolate pretzels and servings of seven cheese pizza on every piece of furniture in the room. There was such a crowd in the room I was trapped there for an hour. You know— I'm talking, I'm eating, I'm eating, I'm talking.

## THE CURSE OF CHEESE WHIZ

I think this whole holiday pattern of "grazing" at house parties has come about because of Cheese Whiz. When I was growing up in the 1950s holiday party fare consisted of a couple bowls of homemade Chex Mix, a large cooked ham, baskets of bread, pickles and Christmas tree shaped butter cookies. If it was a really fancy party, the hostess might serve green olives and dainty egg salad sandwiches made from Wonder Bread cut into one inch by three inch lengths along with the ham.

That was the tradition in my town. No matter whose house you went to during the holidays you got the same things. Oh, once in a while someone daring would put out a turkey instead of the ham, but that was about the extent of exotic changes at these types of affairs.

I think the world would have kept on going in that mode forever if it hadn't been for the invention of Cheese Whiz in the aerosol can. Before the invention of Cheese Whiz, if anyone wanted to do any fancy hors d'oeuvres for the holidays, they had to start making them in September because in those days everything was handmade. Things like fancy swirls, rosebuds and decorative designs on food usually required you be at least a better-than-average cake decorator or alternately a skilled surgeon.

Then Cheese Whiz came along and suddenly anyone could shake a can could make cracker canopies. Everywhere you went there were trays and trays of Cheese Whiz covered Ritz crackers, bread sticks, melba toast, celery sticks and Christmas-tree shaped butter cookies. Everything looked and tasted great with Cheese Whiz on it. It got to the point that no great party was complete without at least 30 cans of Cheese Whiz on hand. People began decorating their homes with the stuff.

Then one day some Martha Stewart prototype in our town discovered you could melt the cheese and put it in a bowl and people would dip their own cheese whiz. From there, the Christmas party food wars escalated as one party giver tried to outdo each other until today you just can't go to a party without finding a hundred different things you wouldn't normally eat even if you were a Frenchman.

All of this flashed through my mind while I stood at home with the empty bottle of Pepto Abysmal in hand as my wife stood by waiting for the answer as to why I ate so much at the party. I finally looked at her and gave a truthful answer.

"It tasted good."

*Why women intentionally decide to make things the day before Christmas with ingredients that can only be gotten through barter with Moroccan spice merchants is beyond me.*

## SURVIVING CHRISTMAS BAKING

After weeks of hectic preparation, it's hard to believe we have finally arrived at Christmas Eve and can relax.

Having bought all of my Christmas presents at pre-Thanksgiving, post-Halloween sales in October, there will be no last-minute shopping trips for me this year. It will actually seem kind of strange to be able to get up on Christmas Eve morning and not have to run around from store-to-store, fighting in hand-to-hand combat with other husbands and fathers over the last broken toy and irregular-size women's bib overalls so we can show our love for our kids and spouses.

But just because I have all of my Christmas buying done doesn't mean I'm through shopping. From past experience, I know with time on my hands and no football on the TV, I will become the designated "gopher" for the day, as in "Honey, I'm out of cream cheese and walnuts for the Christmas cookies I'm baking. Can you go for them?"

Even though I'll probably be ensconced in my cushy reclining chair watching "It's a Wonderful Life" for the 37th time this season when my wife asks that question, as a dutiful husband, I cannot refuse on Christmas Eve to go out and bring home the necessary ingredients of Christmas cookies. Except, it won't just be walnuts and cream cheese on the list — things I can find with ease. The list will also include such incomprehensible things as biscotti, cilantro and, of course, "chutney."

I know there is no point in asking why we need these things because the answer will be the inevitable, "It's for Christmas baking."

# HUSBANDS ARE HUNTERS

Why women intentionally decide to make things the day before Christmas with ingredients that can only be gotten through barter with Moroccan spice merchants is beyond me. The only thing less logical is sending their husbands out to find these things.

The reason they do this is because if they asked one of the kids to go out in search of the same ingredients, our boys would just go down to the local 7-Eleven store and read magazines for two hours before coming back home to report they couldn't find the stuff.

Husbands, on the other hand—hunters from prehistoric times—will go, "Sure dear, I'll go out and track down some cumin and phillo dough for you. No problem," and then try to find anything remotely resembling those words.

Last year, I went on one of the Christmas Eve day ingredient hunts. The store, Fred and Bubba's Shoppe and Bag, was full of wild-eyed husbands pushing their shopping carts aimlessly through the store, going "Grueyere. Does anyone know where I can find two pounds of Grueyere?"

One burly guy with tattoos accosted me as soon as I entered the store. "You look like someone who would know where to find pine nuts," he said. "I'll give you two new truck tires if you can find me a box of pine nuts."

Now, if women would only ask us guys to go to the store and find a 11/16th socket, "Gunk" or "Liquid Wrench," we'd know exactly where to look and be back in five minutes. But no man has a clue where to even begin looking for Marzipan.

Sometimes, as a guy, you have to improvise. Like once when my wife wanted "sesame seeds" for bread, I just bought four dozen sesame bagels, scraped the seeds off into a plastic bag and threw away the bagels. I was done in half the time it would have taken to find the real thing.

The only guys in the store on Christmas Eve who know what they're looking for, and where to find it, are the single guys. You can always tell single guys in the grocery store at Christmas time. They're usually pushing a cart full of beer, with one pound of baloney and a box of day-old doughnuts, going, "That should hold me through New Year's."

## WHAT'S PROSCIUTTO?

The married guys, on the other hand, look like Zombies stumbling into displays of canned mandarin oranges and tripping over one another while trying to decipher words like "shiitake" and "prosciutto" from cryptic handwritten notes their wives gave them. Sometimes, I think women just make these things up to drive us crazy. During last year's trip, I came across one guy sitting on the floor in the middle of frozen foods, hugging his knees, rocking back and forth like a little child.

"What's a matter, fellow?" I asked, patting him gently on the head, while trying not to make any sudden moves that might startle him.

"I can't find the stuff on my wife's shopping list," he said, holding out a crumpled piece of paper between clenched fingers. I pried the note from his hands and looked at the words scrawled on the paper. It read, "Two packages of Topo Gigo."

"Do you know what that is?" he asked, pleading for help with his eyes.

"If I'm not mistaken, buddy, I think Topo Gigo is a little mouse puppet that used to appear on the old Ed Sullivan Show," I said. He looked at me dumbfounded. "Does that mean I can't buy it here?"

I felt sorry for him, so I took his list and scratched out Topo Gigo and wrote in "tapioca," then pointed him toward the pudding aisle. "Go for it," I said, as he skipped off merrily down the aisle.

I, on the other hand, spent an hour wandering the store with about 200 other guys without any luck. Deciding to put my organizational skills to work, I called together all the men in the store and made them a proposition.

"Gentlemen, the situation is hopeless," I began. " We have no more hope of finding Tarragon than we do Anisette oil.

"Now, we can either wander around the store all day, or we can simply beg the next woman who walks in the store to find these things for us,'" I suggested. Everybody liked the idea and the next lady who walked in the store—a sweet kindly grand-motherly type—took pity on us.

"I'll help you," she said, "but I've got to warn you, I'm not as quick on my feet as I used to be." With that, she headed off into the store with our lists. Six minutes later, she delivered everything to the counter.

I went home that night and presented my wife with the complete cargo of baking supplies she had sent me for, including the chutney. She was pleased, but she had forgotten one things.

"I still need a quarter pound of Topo Gigo. Could you go to the store for it?"

*While most families have memories about lovely, snowy*
*Christmas morns with sleepy-eyed young ones*
*awakening to a bounty of gifts under the tree*
*from Santa, our Christmas stories seem*
*to fall more in the "strange*
*but true" category.*

# SURVIVING CHRISTMAS MEMORIES

I've always found the Christmas holiday season to be a time of wonder and amazement.

Each year, I wonder how we're going to pay for it, and I'm amazed we're still solvent on New Year's Day.

Quite frankly, I don't know how things got so out of hand. I can remember our first Christmas, when there was just the two of us. My wife, Madeline, and I, poor as church mice, were living in an attic apartment with no money for Christmas presents.

Madeline had beautiful long auburn locks in those days, and I wanted to get her silver combs for her hair for Christmas. So I pawned my gold pocket watch to buy the combs, only to find she had cut off her long auburn hair and sold it to buy me a gold watch chain.

"That was pretty dumb," I remember saying." Now, I've got no watch and you're bald."

I'm sure hundreds of other people have Christmas memories like that.

That's what makes Christmas so special, those golden moments, locked in time, that you can remember and retell your kids every year until they yell, "Stop! Not the hairy watch chain story again."

## STRANGE BUT TRUE CHRISTMASES

Actually, our family collects Christmas stories year-to-year like some people save wrapping paper. My wife and I started it, and now it's become sort of a collective oral history of our

Christmases past. While most families have memories about lovely, snowy Christmas morns with sleepy-eyed young ones awakening to a bounty of gifts under the tree from Santa Claus, our Christmas stories seem to fall more in the "strange but true" category.

Take for example our Christmas tree stories. I'm sure everybody out there has a favorite story about the time the dog got drunk, and knocked over the Christmas tree. Ours get more bizarre than that.

One of our most unforgettable Christmas tree stories was the year of the smelly Christmas tree. That year, he-man that I am, I went out to the woods and cut this tree by hand. Once back and decorated, the tree began to give off an aroma that was a cross between moose droppings and old gym socks.

Not wanting to undecorate the tree, throw it out and go buy another Christmas tree, I did the next best thing. I went out and purchased a whole bunch of those evergreen-scented car deodorizers and hung them on the tree.

With the pine sent of artificial chemicals filling the air, I thought I had the odor problem licked until my mother came over and asked why our house smelled like the inside of a '68 Buick.

We topped that tree story a few years later with the time we had to buy two Christmas trees.

That Christmas, I had purchased a freshly cut Michigan pine tree, decorated it, and then watched as the tree turned to campfire tinder over the next two weeks.

I kept saying, "It will last till Christmas. It will last till Christmas."

But even I had to give up on it when the fire department started parking its trucks outside our house and Smokey the Bear showed up at our door for a courtesy call.

Then, there was the year we got the tree with the gypsy moth cocoons that hatched and ate all our house plants.

But we haven't had these problems for a long time now. Not since I stopped buying our trees at Fred and Bubba's Used Tree Lot.

## CHRISTMAS PRESENT MEMORIES

Christmas trees are only a part of our favorite Yuletide stories. We also have great memories of some of the presents we've exchanged over the years.

One year, my wife and I decided to be crafty and make our own Christmas gifts for each other.

She crocheted a beautiful, tan sweater that three, good-sized men could fit into comfortably. I made her a bookcase that fell over every time the phone rang.

That was also the year we bought the kids pre-broken toys. One child got a tricycle with only two wheels and the other got a racing car set that wouldn't race. It was only after the toys were unwrapped and the deficiencies exposed did I read the boxes they came in. On the outside was clearly printed: "Some parts not included. Good Luck."

Anyway, my son, Jason, bless him, gamely carried the two- wheeled tricycle from room-to-room under his arm, happy as a clam. Our other son, Nathan, though, wouldn't stop complaining about the broken racing set. People would ask him what he got for Christmas and he would tell them, "My folks got me a broken racing set." In fact, he started going door-to-door telling the neighbors all he got for Christmas was this broken racing set. A few of them started a toy drive for our house.

But my next-door neighbor saved Christmas by hot wiring the race cars so they would run. I think he did a little something extra while he was at it because I've never seen a slot car do 100-miles-an-hour on a dining room table.

The race cars were pretty neat down the straightaway, but those babies just couldn't handle the turns. Have you ever seen a slot car hit a dining room wall at 100 mph? We call that the "Christmas of new plaster."

## OUR FAVORITE CHRISTMAS

But, I think the all-time favorite memory of Christmas that my wife and I have was the first Christmas we were married.

It was Christmas Eve and our first holiday away from our homes and our family. Snow had fallen all day, turning our little town into a wintry Christmas village.

Huge flakes of the feathery snow were still falling as we drove home from midnight Christmas service, immersed in our private thoughts of loved ones we missed.

As we reached the edge of town, we saw up ahead a lone figure trudging through the snow. It was a man in a Santa Claus suit and white beard with a big sack on his back.

As we rolled down the window to wave to him, he brightened our lonely Christmas when he called out: "Merry Christmas to all, and to all a good night."

"That's all folks."

Additional books
To order copies of this book and other
Lockport books call 1-866-296-2942
or by fax at 1-616-399-2949